Pastor Rosen—

You are a breath
of fresh air — May the
Lord keep blessing you
in His service — Remember it
Jesus is Lord & it could be
today!

D1173577

Sound the Trumpets

Jimmy DeYoung

Sound the Trumpets

Fourth Printing-2003

ISBN 0-9708246-0-2
All Scripture references are from
The Holy Bible, King James Version

Contents

Trend 1: *Aliya*

Trend 2: *Alignment*

Foreword

In one way or another, we are reminded daily that we live in an "information age." Yet despite this proliferation of information, there is a growing frustration over the secular media's pronounced lack of credibility and responsibility in reporting the news. Nowhere is this fact more evident than in their coverage of events taking place in Israel and the Middle East. All too often, misinformation and out-and-out propaganda have replaced fair and objective journalism. Consequently, an anti-Israel bias is growing around the globe. And if left unchecked, it will produce serious consequences for Israel, the Jewish people, and ultimately, for the world.

In "Sound the Trumpets," Jimmy DeYoung brings two indispensable elements together. As an experienced journalist, he accurately reports the facts concerning what is taking place in Israel and surrounding countries. But of even greater importance to Bible-believing Christians, he provides a Biblical and prophetic perspective on the events now shaping history.

For years Jimmy's preaching, radio reports, and videos have enlightened and encouraged millions of people. Now, with "Sound the Trumpets," believers will have another valuable resource. With history sliding rapidly toward its inevitable conclusion, to say this book is timely is certainly an understatement. I'm sure you will agree as you read "Sound the Trumpets."

ELWOOD MCQUAID
Executive Director
The Friends of Israel

Acknowledgements

No work of this kind is possible without the help of some very special people. I would like to express my heartfelt gratitude to the following individuals who helped me complete this volume:

My wife, Judy, who has always been such an encouragement to me, on this and other projects.

Mart DeHaan, President of RBC Ministries, who has allowed me the privilege of co-teaching with him on the Day of Discovery television program. Mart also spent many hours talking with me about the contents of this book.

Dr. Elwood McQuaid, Executive Director of Friends of Israel, who is a partner in ministry to present the prophetic truths of God's Word. His advice and encouragement to write on this subject were needed to complete the project.

Rick DeYoung, my son, who did much of the research on this book and has managed the publication process.

Sara DeYoung, my daughter-in-law, who, in addition to research, typed the manuscript in its various forms.

Mrs. Winnie Mattheiss, who offered guidance and advice during various stages in development of the manuscript.

And last, but not least, Mrs. Bonnie Varble, who offered help and valuable suggestions in the editing and publishing of this book.

JIMMY DEYOUNG

Chapter 1
Trends of the Times

The shrill sound of the siren broke the silence of the still night air over Jerusalem. Warning of an incoming Scud, the siren startled my wife, Judy, and me from a sound sleep. Awakening to the realization that Iraqi dictator Saddam Hussein had launched an attack, we hurried from our bedroom and ran toward the "sealed room."

The sealed room was a room in our apartment that we had previously prepared in anticipation of just such an attack. The room was set up to keep us from harm should one of those Scud missiles be carrying a biological or chemical warhead. A few days earlier we had readied the room by covering each window with three sheets of plastic, removing all pictures from the walls, and plastering over any nail holes. In addition to these fortifications, we had stockpiled supplies in the sealed room—glass containers filled with water and cans filled with food—in the event outside conditions deteriorated and we were forced into a lengthy stay.

As we ran into the sealed room, I began to put the finishing touches on sealing the door behind us. Judy and I had run a few practice drills the day before, so I knew exactly what I needed to do and I was focused on the task at hand. Suddenly, my concentration was broken. Above the shrill siren blast, I heard a ringing noise. It was the telephone. It was 2 a.m., there was an incoming Scud approaching our apartment, and the telephone was ringing! We had only been in Jerusalem four days. Who in the world was calling?

I rushed to the phone to find out it was our youngest daughter, Jodi, calling from Chattanooga,

Tennessee. Jodi informed me that she had been watching CNN and the newscasters were reporting a Scud coming to Jerusalem from Iraq. "Jodi, I know that. I have to go." Slamming the phone down, I ran to join Judy and sealed the door behind us. As we sat there, with gas masks on, we were certain that Saddam Hussein's missile launchers in Iraq were targeted directly upon our modest apartment in the City of Jerusalem.

Over the next five hours, we learned to communicate with one another through the gas masks. Of course, we were very much concerned. It was the first time we had ever been in this type of situation. We were under attack by an enemy of the Jewish people. Most of the five hours we spent in prayer, but we also had time to meditate upon what had been taking place just recently in Israel.

Four Major Trends

As journalists stationed in Jerusalem, we were very much aware that this was a time of great "aliya." "Aliya" is the Hebrew word that Biblically means, "to go up to Jerusalem." Today the term "aliya" is used to refer to immigration.

In January 1991 a great exodus of Jewish people out of the former Soviet Union had started to take place. Ultimately, over 890,000 Jews from that region would emigrate and make aliya to Israel. During the Gulf Crisis, however, as we sat in our sealed room, awaiting an incoming Scud from an enemy of Israel, I thought about all of those Russian Jews. The Russian Jews, fleeing the Soviet Union to escape their problems, were now faced with the problem of actually staying alive.

As you might expect, five hours in a sealed room

allowed us time to think about more than just the new Jewish immigrants arriving from the former Soviet Union. I was reminded that nations were forming coalitions. The United States government had formed a coalition of nations to fight Saddam Hussein and his aggressive acts against Kuwait. The coalition was aware of Saddam's desires to attack and take control of Saudi Arabia, as well.

In addition to the coalition formed by the United States, Great Britain, and other nations of the West, there was an alignment of nations in the Arab world who were a part of the Western-world alignment of nations. Egypt, Syria, and Lebanon had not joined with Saddam Hussein, but with the Western coalition instead. Jordan, with the longest Arab-Israeli border, had joined forces with Saddam Hussein.

Many in the Arab world, including the Palestinians, rushed to their rooftops every time a siren broke the silence of the Israeli sky, and prayed that the Scud would hit the Jewish people. They wanted Saddam to have the victory over the Jewish occupation of the land. These Arab nations, whether aligned with the United States or Iraq, wanted the "Israel problem" to be taken care of through this Gulf Crisis.

Another thought that crossed our minds as we sat there was about all of the work that had been going on in an effort to establish a comprehensive peace in the Middle East. Anticipation for peace was prevalent all over the world, especially after the agreement at Camp David, which developed into the Camp David Accords. Supposedly, peaceful relationships between the largest Arab country, Egypt, and the Jewish people of Israel had been accomplished.

Equally encouraging were other tracks that had opened up in the peace effort. The Israelis were secretly meeting with the Palestinians, endeavoring to put together an agreement between the Palestinians and the Israelis. At the same time, there were secret talks being held with the Syrians by the Israelis. The Arab world was seeking peace with a nation whom they did not even recognize as a sovereign state in our world.

I found out later that during the thirty-nine times when the warning sirens sounded across Israel, telling of an incoming Scud, most of the Orthodox Jewish community who lived in the Old City of Jerusalem did not put on their gas masks. Instead of putting on their gas masks and running quickly to their sealed rooms, they left their homes and went immediately to the Western Wall, where they started to pray.

Their prayer during this time of trouble was the same prayer that they offer up daily; in fact, three times each day. They pray for the building of the temple. The temple that they pray for is to stand, one day, on the sacred and holy Temple Mount. Preparations for this coming temple, prophesied by the Prophet Ezekiel, are being made today by many in the Orthodox Jewish community.

There is, however, one major problem. The actual location where they are to build the temple is occupied by the Moslem Dome of the Rock. The prayers of these dedicated Orthodox Jews were lifted to God requesting that He would allow one of these incoming Scuds to actually hit the Dome of the Rock, clearing the area so that they could start construction on their temple.

We had five hours of anxiety, sitting in our sealed room, anticipating the possibility of a Scud delivering a chemical or biological warhead to the City of Jerusalem. Finally, another siren broke through the silent skies of the early morning sunrise over Jerusalem to communicate an "all-clear" signal to those of us who had been awake all night, anticipating a disastrous missile strike on the Jewish state.

As we sat for five hours in that sealed room, with gas masks over our faces, we found ourselves stunned by the possibility that we were actually experiencing a last-days conflict predicted long ago by the prophets of Israel. While there is no way of knowing how much time is left on God's calendar, we sensed that we were witnessing, with our own eyes, events that are setting the stage for the return of Jesus Christ to this earth.

In the following pages, I'd like to share with you four trends that can be seen in the world today. Foretold by ancient Biblical prophets, these trends reveal to us that the end times are near. The reality of these trends gives me reason to believe that the human race is living just moments away from the Rapture of the Church. This thrilling event could happen next week; it could happen tomorrow; it could happen today. Christians should be ready for the Lord's return, and waiting for what I call the "any moment sound of the trumpets."

Chapter 2
God's Unique Instrument

As we sat through thirty-nine siren blasts, each warning of an incoming Scud, I thought of how man, today, uses the instrument of an air-raid siren to sound an alert, just as God, in Biblical times, used the trumpet to warn His people of immediate danger. God used the trumpet not only to warn His people, but also to direct the Jews to His desired goals for them. Soon, God will sound the trumpet again, to gather His people.

In Biblical times, the trumpet that was used to sound the alert or call attention was made from a ram's horn. Known as a "shofar" in Hebrew, its origin, by Jewish tradition, comes from an incident that took place on Mount Moriah some four thousand years ago. Genesis 22 describes how Abraham went up on the mount (which is today the Temple Mount in the Old City of Jerusalem) and offered his only son, Isaac, as a sacrifice. As Abraham stretched forth his hand, taking his knife to slay his son, suddenly the *"angel of the Lord"*—probably a pre-incarnate appearance of Jesus Christ—called to Abraham out of Heaven and said, *"Abraham,...Here am I....Lay not thine hand upon the lad, neither do thou any thing unto him"* (Genesis 22:11-12).

Abraham, as he lifted up his eyes, saw a ram caught in a thicket by his horns. Abraham took hold of the ram and offered him for a burnt offering instead of his son. Jewish tradition says that the shofar, a simple trumpet made from a ram's horn, was thereafter established as an instrument that God would use to direct His people, to call a sacred assembly of His people, to gather His people, and to warn them of imminent danger.

While Hebrew references to the shofar have been translated as "trumpet" in modern versions of the Bible, we can find the first usage of the shofar in the Scriptures in Exodus 19. Moses and the Israelites were camped in the valley at the base of Mount Sinai. Just prior to giving Moses the Ten Commandments—the Jewish law—God sounded the shofar to warn the people that He was getting ready to communicate to Moses (Exodus 19:16). So loud was the sound of the shofar that the people in the camp trembled. Then in verse 19, God called Moses to Him with the *"voice of the trumpet"* (shofar). It sounded long and waxed louder and louder until Moses spoke to the Lord. Then the Lord answered back and came down and Moses went up to meet Him there on Mount Sinai (verse 20). Thus, the shofar was used to call Moses up to meet the Lord.

The blowing of the shofar was the responsibility of the priests even after the wilderness journey was over and the tribes were settled in the land. The trumpets would be blown particularly in times of war. The role of the priests in combat and the Lord's promise to respond to the trumpets suggested that His people were to be involved in holy war. They were to fight the battles of the Lord as they led the way against the enemies and guaranteed success.

The priests were also to blow the trumpets at the times of the major feasts, which included Passover, Feast of Unleavened Bread, Feast of Weeks, Feast of Pentecost, and Feast of Tabernacles. This blowing of the trumpets was not so much to announce these various festivals, as it was to invoke and celebrate the presence of God among His people.

God Himself, in effect, was said to be in the long blast of these priestly shofars: *"Lift up your heads, O ye gates; and be ye lifted up, ye everlasting doors; and the King of glory shall come in"* (Psalm 24:7). When Christ returns, He, the King of Glory, will enter cities in triumph.

In Isaiah 18:3, the prophet talks about the shofar being blown so that the people—the *"inhabitants of the world,"* the *"dwellers on the earth"*—would be gathered together. Also, in Isaiah 27:13, it says that in that day the great shofar *"shall be blown, and they shall come."* It describes the entire world that will gather on the holy mount in Jerusalem. The shofar will be used to gather the Jewish people from the entire world to the City of Jerusalem on the Temple Mount.

Blowing of the shofar also relates to the end times. This is evident when the Lord says, *"Blow ye the [shofar] in [Jerusalem], and sound an alarm in my holy mountain: let all the inhabitants of the land tremble: for the day of the Lord cometh, for it is nigh at hand"* (Joel 2:1). This is, in fact, a prophecy dealing with the end times when the shofar will be used to gather the people into the land of Israel to be ready to battle.

The air-raid warning siren was sounded to alert the Israelis, and those of us who were living in Israel at the time of the Gulf Crisis, of an incoming Scud. So the shofar—or trumpet—will sound the alert to gather all of the Jewish people at the time of the Second Coming.

Chapter 3
Sound the Trumpets

On a recent trip into the foothills of the Great Smoky Mountains, in Eastern Tennessee and Western North Carolina, Judy and I drove through Pigeon Forge, Tennessee, on our way to Gatlinburg and then up into the Smokies. As we approached the city of Pigeon Forge, we were totally amazed by the number of Christmas lights decorating the buildings and even the trees that line the parking lots.

As we made our way through this winter wonderland to the hotel where I was to speak at a prophecy conference, all of a sudden, I could no longer contain myself, and I shouted, "Boy, I can't wait. Thanksgiving is almost here!"

My excitement was that Thanksgiving brings our family together at Judy's mother's home in Tallahassee, Florida, for that great traditional dinner with all the trimmings. Judy turned, looked at me, and asked, "What do you mean, 'Thanksgiving is almost here?' Why did you say that? How did you know Thanksgiving is almost here?" My response was, "Well, I know Thanksgiving is almost here because I can see the signs for Christmas, and I know that Thanksgiving comes before Christmas."

Indeed, many signs were evident to tell us that we were entering the Christmas season. My statement was based upon my knowledge that Thanksgiving comes before Christmas; if the signs indicated that Christmas was so close, then how much closer must Thanksgiving be.

A Biblical End-Time Scenario

That same principle works as well when you think about the Rapture of the Church, that time when Jesus will call up all believers to be with Him, to be forever in His presence. The Rapture comes before a terrible time of trouble called "the seventieth week of Daniel" or the "Tribulation Period." This Tribulation, a seven-year period of time, will end with the Revelation of Jesus Christ, at which time He will come back to the earth to establish His Kingdom. As we see the signs for the approaching Tribulation and subsequent Revelation of Jesus Christ, then how much closer must the Rapture be?

That end-time scenario, according to the Bible, is as follows:

1. *Rapture of the Church*

   The next event on God's calendar of events for the last days is the Rapture of the Church (I Thessalonians 4:13-18). This event could take place at any moment. There are no signs needed for it to happen; no prophecies are yet to be fulfilled.

2. *Tribulation Period*

   Then there will be a seven-year period of time known as the Great Tribulation (described in Revelation 4:2–19:10). Also referred to as "the seventieth week of Daniel" or "the time of Jacob's trouble," this period of great suffering will not begin until after the Rapture of the Church.

3. *Revelation of Jesus Christ*

   The Second Coming of Jesus is next (Revelation 19:11-21). Also referred to as the Revelation of Christ or the Return of

Christ. This event will take place when Jesus actually comes all the way back to earth, stepping down on the Mount of Olives in Jerusalem (Zechariah 14:4).

A Sign Or A Sound?

As we look at the signs or trends that will be discussed in this book, notice that I Corinthians 1:22 says that the signs are for the Jewish people. Christians are not looking for signs, because there are no signs or events that must take place before the Rapture. Next, for the Christian, will be the sound of the trumpet that will call all believers to come to be with Christ.

But, as we wait to hear that trumpet blast, we can't help but see the trends unfolding that provide those signs which God promised to give to the Jewish people; signs of the Revelation of Jesus Christ, His return to the earth. And it's the presence of these trends that makes us aware of the time in which we are living. As we examine the shadows that they cast back, we can certainly conclude that the Rapture seems to be very close at hand.

As introduced in the previous chapter, God's musical instrument, the shofar (trumpet), will call together all Christians to be with Jesus Christ at the Rapture. Then, at least seven years later, the trumpet will sound a second time, for Jewish and Gentile believers from the Tribulation and all other periods of time (except those of the Church Age, who were taken at the Rapture to be with Christ). This second trumpet sound will be used to gather the Gentile and Jewish believers together, both living and dead, from every corner of the earth and from out of the Third Heaven itself to Him in Jerusalem.

These two trumpet sounds, the trumpet that will sound for the Rapture of the Church and the trumpet that will sound heralding the Return of Christ, are at this point in time still future events. I must remind you, these are two distinctly different sounds, at two diversely different times.

The Trumpet Sounds

First, there is the sound of the trumpet that calls for the Church. At the time of Christ's return for His saints, it will be announced from Heaven forcefully and dramatically with the sound of the trumpet. This is recorded in I Thessalonians 4:16. This trumpet sound will be accompanied by a shout from Jesus Christ and the shout of the archangel. These three phenomena could all refer to the same sound, but probably they are three separate, simultaneous sounds used by the Lord to call His Church to be with Him.

In a separate letter, found in I Corinthians 15:50-58, the Apostle Paul revealed this Biblical truth to the people of Corinth: the "mystery" of the Rapture of the Church is that the dead in Christ will first be raised and then the living will be instantaneously transformed and caught up to meet Him in the air.

The trumpet, in Old Testament times, signaled the appearance of God. The trumpet that will sound at the Rapture of the Church will signal the appearance of Jesus Christ. In Paul's letters to both the Corinthians and the Thessalonians, he reveals that the trumpet at the Rapture will not only signal Christ's appearance, but our departure to be with Him.

The trumpet sound at the time of the Rapture is referred to as the *"last trump"* (I Corinthians 15:52). It is the last trumpet blast for the Church because this appearance of Christ will never end. By the way, there is no basis for pre-tribulationists equating this last trumpet with the seventh trumpet judgment found in Revelation 11:15-19. The trumpet judgments in Revelation pertain to judgments during the Tribulation, whereas the "last trump" in I Corinthians 15 is related to the Church and the call at the time of the Rapture to gather Christians to be with Jesus Christ, before the Tribulation Period begins.

There are several reasons why you cannot equate the "last trump" of I Corinthians 15:52 with the "trumpet judgments" in Revelation. First, it will not be the final trump. There will be another trumpet sound (Matthew 24:31), when Jesus has His angels blow the trumpet to gather all the Jewish and Gentile believers from every part of the universe. This trumpet sounding takes place after the seven trumpet judgments, at the Revelation of Christ.

Second, the last trump in I Corinthians 15 is a time of blessing, not a time of judgment as in the seven trumpet judgments in Revelation. With the sound of the trumpet at the Rapture, Christians enter their eternal reward, greeted by none other than Jesus Christ Himself. The seventh, or last, trumpet judgment does not bring blessing. Instead, this "last trumpet" leads into the seven vial judgments (Revelation 16), before the Lord returns. These vial judgments are worse than the trumpet judgments.

There is a third reason that confirms these are two entirely different trumpet sounds. It takes quite a period of time for the seven trumpet judgments to unfold here on the earth during the Tribulation. As just mentioned, the vial judgments come out of the seventh trumpet judgment. Though the vials happen quickly, they are not as quick as the "last trump" of I Corinthians 15.

This *"last trump"* is a very quick happening. *"In a moment, in the twinkling of an eye,"* this trumpet sound goes forth (I Corinthians 15:52).

We must conclude that the trumpet sound referred to in I Thessalonians 4:16 and I Corinthians 15:52 will be the trumpet blast that will call the Church to be with Jesus Christ. From that time forward, the Church will never leave His presence again throughout eternity.

The "Church" is that group of individuals who have come to know Jesus Christ as Lord and Saviour during the time period between the Resurrection of Jesus Christ and the Rapture of the Church. This eschatological event, the Rapture, is that which takes place prior to the beginning of the Tribulation, that seven years of terrible trouble before the actual return of Jesus Christ back to earth.

At prophecy conferences and in prophecy books we learn about many signs that point to the soon coming of Jesus Christ. These are not signs for the Rapture of the Church. Remember the Church is not looking for signs but is, in fact, listening for a sound. The signs will precede the Return of Christ to the earth. These signs will warn the Jews and Gentiles left on the earth after the Rapture of the days in which they are living, prior to the Return of Christ.

The next sound of a trumpet, after the Tribulation, will be for blessing and not for judgment. It will be the trumpet sounded after the one that is blown for the Rapture of the Church. It will be the one that will gather a people, the Jewish people, together to be with Jesus Christ in Jerusalem. It will be blown, as recorded in the Book of Matthew, when Jesus Christ comes back to the earth, planting His feet on the Mount of Olives. He will then send His *"angels with a great sound of a trumpet, and they shall gather together his elect from the four winds, from one end of heaven to the other"*; from all over the world, all over Heaven, all over creation (Matthew 24:31).

God will use the sound of a trumpet to call the Jewish people to come to the holy Temple Mount in Jerusalem. Therefore, the sound of a trumpet, God's musical instrument, will be once again used to direct His people to the location that He wants them to gather for a solemn assembly. It will call attention to God Himself, this sound of the trumpet.

I believe we are quickly approaching these two trumpet sounds and the events that they will proclaim—the first trumpet signaling the Rapture of the Church; the second trumpet heralding the Return of Christ back to the earth for the regathering of the Jewish people to Jerusalem. My belief is based on Biblical prophecy, which reveals four major trends that will occur before the second trumpet blast. These trends, which I see today unfolding on this earth, serve as indicators for the upcoming end-time events.

My story about the Christmas lights or the signs of Christmas showing me evidence of the soon coming of Thanksgiving has an interesting relationship to the Rapture. The four trends mentioned in Chapter 1, which will happen during the last days, alert us to the closeness of His coming. These four trends will culminate during the Tribulation Period. As we see the signs for the sound of the second trumpet of Matthew 24:31, our attention should be drawn to the fact that the sound of the first trumpet of I Thessalonians 4:16 can only be closer at hand.

Trends Before The Trumpet

Four major trends lead up to the sounding of the second trumpet: aliya of the Jewish people; alignment of the nations; anticipation of peace; and arrangements for the temple. The Hebrew word "aliya" is now being applied to the actions of those people who are immigrating to Israel, coming from all over the world making their way back to Jerusalem.

The second trend is the alignment of the nations. This alignment involves nations joining forces against the Jewish people in an effort to remove them from the Middle East and the land that God has given them. Further, many of these hostile countries have a burning desire to eradicate the Jews from the face of the earth.

The third trend that is prevalent today, giving us evidence of the soon coming of Jesus Christ, is the anticipation of peace. When we speak of peace, we speak of a peace on a worldwide scale. But, in reality, when we think of peace, we think of peace in the Middle East; peace between the Jewish people of Israel and their Arab neighbors. Thousands and thousands of man-hours have been spent in efforts to bring about this peace. The leaders of nations, in particular the leader of the most powerful country of the world, the United States, seem to work tirelessly to bring about peace. Presidents, past and present, have done all that they can to bring about peace in the Middle East. The word "peace" is on the lips of so many of us around the world. Anticipation for that peace is a great indicator of how close we may be to the Return of Jesus Christ.

The fourth trend that is also present in Jerusalem today is arrangements for the temple. I have spoken with every personality and investigated every project involved in preparation to build the next temple. As we consider this later in this book, we will see that preparations for that temple are basically complete. The Bible tells us in Daniel 9:27, that there will be a temple standing on the Temple Mount in Jerusalem during the coming Tribulation Period. Arrangements for that temple are in the final stages and the erection of the temple could be very close.

These four major trends—aliya of the Jewish people, alignment of the nations, anticipation of peace, and arrangements for the temple—give us evidence of how soon those trumpets could be sounded. Remember, the first trumpet is to call up the Church to be with Christ. Then the Tribulation Period unfolds here on earth with these four major trends coming to a climax. After that, the second trumpet will sound to gather all believers to Jerusalem where Jesus Christ will rule and reign.

TREND 1
Aliya

Chapter 4
Aliya of the Jewish People

The big 747 cruises over the Mediterranean coast in its approach to Ben-Gurion International Airport. As the passenger jet touches down on the tarmac, the excitement is almost uncontrollable in the hearts and lives of the Christian pilgrims. They, for the first time, have just caught a glimpse of a land that they've read about for so many years: Israel.

Everybody rushes into the bus that stands ready to take these newly arrived passengers to passport control, where they get their visa for a short-term visit in the land of the Bible. After collecting their baggage, these new arrivals are met by an Israeli guide who loads them onto the air-conditioned tour bus. The guide will travel with them throughout their tour of the Bible land.

This pilgrimage offers a unique opportunity for these believers who have come half-way around the world to visit the Holy Land. It gives them a chance to see Israel past, to touch Israel present, and to visualize Israel future. These three events will come together in an emotional experience that is hard to describe.

As the bus now turns out of Ben-Gurion Airport heading up Highway 1, the highway between Tel Aviv and Jerusalem, the Israeli guide welcomes everyone to Israel for their very first visit. He tells the people that they are on their way "up to Jerusalem."

They are going to make "aliya" he informs the Christian pilgrims, and then goes on to describe what this Hebrew word means. The literal translation is "going up to Jerusalem," but the Israeli guide reveals that this is a spiritual experience as well, and every Jew that comes to the Holy Land says a special prayer in Hebrew. The guide then recites this Hebrew prayer for the new arrivals.

As they geographically make their way to Jerusalem, starting at sea level at the airport and rising to more than 2,700 feet, they literally do "go *up* to Jerusalem." But, as the Israeli guide pointed out, making aliya means more than just driving up to Jerusalem. For the very first time these people will have the opportunity to see the eternal city, the city that God has chosen for His habitation among His people throughout eternity.

Biblical Aliya

In Old Testament times, the word "aliya" was used to describe the responsibility of the Jewish male who was required to go up to Jerusalem three times each year. The cycle of the Jewish feasts, which God gave the Jewish people, made this a requirement. Three of the seven Jewish feasts were known as "pilgrim" feasts—Passover, Pentecost, and Tabernacles— because the male of the family was required to make his way to Jerusalem to the temple to bring special sacrifices and offerings and to worship there at the temple. Three times each year, the Jewish male made aliya to Jerusalem.

Now, however, the word "aliya" has been made applicable to what we understand as immigration. When the Jewish people, who through the centuries have been dispersed throughout the world, decide to return to the land of their forefathers, their homeland, they make aliya; or, in other words, they immigrate from their present location or nation to the state of Israel.

Aliya is one of the great indicators that Christians

can watch for as they look for trends that will take place prior to the second coming of Jesus Christ. Before and during that seven-year period of time called the Tribulation will be aliya, or immigration of the Jewish people. God has made promises to the Jewish people that He must keep, promises pertaining to the land that will be returned to His people.

Diasporas And Aliyas

When God made these promises, He did so saying He would reach into the world where Jews have been scattered for almost two thousand years and bring them back into their own land, land originally given to their forefathers. Before we get into that subject, however, let's think about the three Diasporas of the Jewish people (dispersions throughout the entire world) and the three aliyas of the Jewish people (returns to their Promised Land).

After Abraham made his way from Ur of the Chaldees, over the Fertile Crescent, and into the land that God had promised to give to him and all of his descendents, problems arose. The descendents of Abraham—his son Isaac and his grandson Jacob— stayed in the land given them until around seventeen hundred years before the birth of Jesus Christ. At that time, Jacob, because of a famine in the Promised Land, took his family, all of their cattle, all of their goods, and all that they had gotten from the land of Canaan, and went into Egypt.

To Egypt And Back

Genesis 46:27 tells us, *"all the souls of the house of Jacob, which came into Egypt, were threescore and ten,"* or seventy people. Seventy members left this beginning Jewish nation. For more than four hundred years they remained in Egyptian bondage until God raised up a man to bring His people out of Egypt. The man who delivered Israel from Egyptian captivity was himself a Hebrew, a man named Moses.

The Bible tells us in Exodus 12, that after four hundred and thirty years of bondage, the Jewish population had grown to 600,000 men, in addition to the women and children. So, approximately two million Jewish people came out of the land of Egypt, out from under Egyptian bondage, and made their way to the Promised Land.

The Lord instructed Moses to take the Israelites to the Promised Land. But they were not allowed to go into the land as they could have, had they had faith and believed God for what He told them He would do. They could have gone into the Promised Land; but because of their lack of faith they were made to wander around for forty years. Finally, Moses passed from the scene and his military leader Joshua took them across the Jordan River and into the land that God had set aside for His people.

To Babylon And Back

The first Diaspora occurred when Jacob took his family into Egypt and then the first aliya, four hundred and seventy years later, occurred when Joshua took the Israelites back into the land. The second Diaspora, or departure, of the Jewish people out of the land that God had given to them into a foreign one is recorded in II Chronicles 36. It was during the third invasion, with military actions, under King Nebuchadnezzar, who was at that time head of the Babylonian Empire.

In 605 B.C., Nebuchadnezzar came down for his first invasion into the land of Israel, taking Daniel, the three Hebrew children and literally thousands of others back into Babylonian captivity. In 597 B.C., he came and took Ezekiel out of the land, with around ten thousand others. Then in 586 B.C., in his third military wave, Nebuchadnezzar went into Israel, devastated the City of Jerusalem, destroyed the temple, and dispersed the Jewish people into Babylonian captivity. Only a handful fled with Jeremiah into Egypt.

Seventy years later, as recorded in Ezra 1–6, God raised up Zerubbabel to lead almost fifty thousand people, (49,897 to be exact) on their return to Jerusalem. Back home in Israel, Zerubbabel led the Jewish people in rebuilding the temple that had been destroyed. Thus ended the second Diaspora of the Jews, from the Babylonian captivity, with Zerubbabel leading them back into the land—the second aliya.

To The World...

The third Diaspora took place in 70 A.D., following the destruction of Herod's Temple and the devastation of the City of Jerusalem. General Titus, leader of the Roman Army, fulfilled the prophecy of Jesus Christ. Jesus, in Matthew 24:1-2, told His disciples as they walked from Herod's Temple that the building would not be left standing: *"There shall not be left here one stone upon another."* Almost forty years to the day that Jesus Christ made that prediction, it was fulfilled, as if Jesus had pre-written the history.

General Titus, who had been on the Mount of Olives with his troops, looking down on Jerusalem, across the Kidron Valley, mentioned this magnificent building, Herod's Temple. This was a structure of which the rabbis had said during this time, "If you have never seen Herod's Temple, you've never seen a beautiful building." In fact, General Titus told his troops that he had traveled in every major city of the world and nothing was as majestic as Herod's Temple.

The Roman Army came across the Kidron Valley, climbed up the Temple Mount, destroyed the temple, devastated Jerusalem, and dispersed the Jews from the land. However, this dispersion differed from the other dispersions. It wasn't to one location, like the first dispersion into Egypt or the second dispersion into Babylon. This time, in fulfillment of the prophecy made by Moses in Deuteronomy 28, the Jews were dispersed into the four corners of the earth.

In Deuteronomy 28:15 and verses that follow, we see where God used His servant Moses, who had been responsible for bringing the people out of the Egyptian bondage on the first aliya and leading them toward the Promised Land, to give a prophecy that relates to the prophecy of Jesus. God gave a special prophecy to Moses, saying that if Israel was obedient and kept His commands, they would receive many blessings.

Verse 15 says, *"But it shall come to pass, if thou wilt not hearken unto the voice of the Lord thy God, to observe to do all his commandments and his statutes which I command thee this day; that all these curses shall come upon thee, and overtake thee"* and they indeed would be dispersed to the four corners of the earth. Verses 63 and 64 say, in part, *"It shall come to pass, that as the Lord rejoiced over you to do you good, and to multiply you; so the Lord will rejoice over you to destroy you, and to bring you to nought; and ye shall be plucked from off the land whither thou goest to possess it. And the Lord shall scatter thee among all people, from the one end of the earth even unto the other."*

He says in verses 65 and 66, *"Among these nations shalt thou find no ease, neither shall the sole of thy foot have rest: but the Lord shall give thee there a trembling heart, and failing of eyes, and sorrow of mind: And thy life shall hang in doubt before thee; and thou shalt fear day and night, and shalt have none assurance of thy life.*" In fact, He says back in verse 37, "*And thou shalt become an astonishment, a proverb, and a byword, among all nations whither the Lord shall lead thee.*" Verse 48 says, "*Therefore shalt thou serve thine enemies.*"

So, because of the disobedience of the Jewish people, the third Diaspora sent them to the four corners of the earth. Then, in chapter 30 of the Book of Deuteronomy, God gives what has been called, the "Palestinian Covenant." This is not a good term to describe this covenant. It should be called the "Covenant of the Land."

God says in Deuteronomy 30:3 that if they shall return to the Lord, "*then the Lord thy God will turn thy captivity, and have compassion upon thee, and will return and gather thee from all the nations, whither the Lord thy God hath scattered thee.*" Verse 5, "*And the Lord thy God will bring thee into the land which thy fathers possessed, and thou shalt possess it; and he will do thee good, and multiply thee above thy fathers.*"

God made another promise through the Prophet Moses. While Moses told the Jewish people that if they weren't obedient to God, they would be dispersed to the four corners of the earth, he also wrote that if they would return to the Lord, He would gather them from all of those nations where they had been scattered and bring them back into the land that He had given to their fathers.

...And Back

The final return to the land has been underway since 1897 with the establishment of the Zionist movement under Theodor Herzl. This third aliya, the third immigration of the Jewish people from around the world, will culminate in the fulfillment of this prophecy.

In the prophecy of Ezekiel 34, God gave Ezekiel a new and different message from the message in the first thirty-two chapters of his book, which had been a message of retribution or judgment that would come upon the Jewish people. In chapter 33, God changes the message. He re-commissioned Ezekiel to give the prophecy of restoration.

Ezekiel's message to the Jewish people is what will happen in the last days. In Ezekiel 34:11-31, God says eighteen times *"I will, I will, I will, I will..."* When we see a phrase repeated that many times, we need to find out why it is there and what He is talking about. In verse 11 He says, *"Thus saith the Lord God; Behold, I, even I, will both search my sheep, and seek them out."* In verse 12, *"So will I seek out my sheep, and will deliver them out of all places where they have been scattered in the cloudy and dark day."*

Verse 13, *"And I will bring them out from the people, and gather them from the countries, and will bring them to their own land, and feed them upon the mountains of Israel by the rivers, and in all the inhabited places of the country."* Verse 14, *"I will feed them in a good pasture."* Verse 15, *"I will feed my flock, and I will cause them to lie down."* Verse 16, *"I will seek that which was lost, and bring again."*

God gives an absolute promise to the Jewish people. If you will return unto me spiritually—becoming obedient to me, honoring me, keeping the statutes that I gave you—I will bring you out of this terrible dispersion. I will gather you from the four corners of the earth and I will bring you back into the land that I promised your forefathers, a land which you will have forever. God has made a promise of an aliya for the

Jewish people.

When you study the Word of God from the Book of Genesis through the Book of Revelation, you will see there are (only) three times that the children of Israel are dispersed from their homeland to some other part of the world: the first time to Egypt, the second time to Babylon, and the third time to the four corners of the earth.

Further study in God's Word reveals that there are only three promises to bring His people back into the land. Three times the Jews will make aliya, thus three times they will be regathered in the land. History tells us that the first time they were gathered out of Egypt under Moses; the second time they were gathered out of Babylon under Zerubbabel, Nehemiah, and Ezra. It is prophesied that the third time, in these last days, they will be regathered from the four corners of the earth. They will return to the land, establishing themselves once again as a nation and, ultimately, they will come to know Jesus Christ as Lord and Saviour.

Chapter 5
Aliya over the Years

One of the joys of living in Jerusalem is to be able to walk down the closed-off pedestrian street called Ben Yehuda Street. It is the street named after Eliazer Ben Yehuda, the man who single-handedly revived the Hebrew language, which is a unique fulfillment of prophecy in itself. Located in the center of Jerusalem, Ben Yehuda Street becomes a virtual crossroad for Israelis who represent almost every nationality in the world.

As you walk down Ben Yehuda Street you'll find that on both sides of the street there are outdoor coffee shops and little cafes where you can stop and have a time of refreshment and fellowship with friends, possibly from the "old country." If you listen closely, you can hear all of the languages of the world spoken here.

I remember when we first arrived in Jerusalem, there was hardly a time that I walked down Ben Yehuda Street when I didn't see someone I knew. Imagine that. In a city of over a half million people, you expect it to be a unique experience to see someone you know. But Jerusalem is a big city with a small-town atmosphere.

Ben Yehuda is a very crowded street. Every Saturday night at the end of the Shabbat (the Jewish Sabbath) people who had been home resting all day will gather there to see friends and enjoy themselves before the new work week starts. On special days, like Independence Day, Ben Yehuda Street is crowded with literally hundreds and thousands of people. On one particular Independence Day, over two hundred thousand people crowded onto this pedestrian walkway.

Just one street over from Ben Yehuda is another

pedestrian street, where restaurants prepare foods for many different nationalities. Both of these pedestrian streets reveal visible evidence of years of immigration, years of aliya, representing over one hundred and twenty-five nations gathered in Jerusalem.

These streets are the "melting-pot" which brings together all these people, from the four corners of the world, into one revived nation. The stories overheard on Ben Yehuda could fill several volumes with the exciting adventures surrounding the return to the Promised Land for the Jewish people.

The Prophetic Return

The return of the Jewish people to modern-day Israel is of utmost prophetic importance. This return is an incredible story that was conceived, planned, and fulfilled all within the last one hundred years. As we examine the miracle of the return, we see the hand of God as He orchestrates world leaders, nations, and forceful personalities to bring about this prophetic event.

Although the modern phenomenon of the return of the Jews has been played out in the last one hundred years, the dream of returning to their ancient homeland began shortly after the Romans dispersed them in the first century. This dispersion, the third Diaspora, displaced the Jewish people from Israel and put them in surrounding areas of the Middle East and Europe.

The Jews who settled in the Middle Eastern countries came to be known as Sephardic Jews while those that made Europe their home were called Ashkenazi Jews. Both groups were continually inspired and motivated by the prospect of a "return to Zion." The literature and art from the Jewish communities of the Middle Ages reflect this longing for the re-establishment of a Jewish homeland.

In the sixteenth and seventeenth centuries a series of Jewish leaders claiming to be "messiahs" came forward to try to convince Jews to return to Israel. These leaders were opposed, however, by the Haskala movement of the late eighteenth century. The Haskala (meaning "Jewish Enlightenment") was an intellectual movement among the Jews of Central and Eastern Europe that encouraged the Jews to assimilate into the Western culture of Europe.

Despite the Haskala, Eastern European Jews did not assimilate. In fact, as a result of organized persecution by the czars of Russia, the Jews formed the *Hovevei Ziyyon* (Lovers of Zion) to promote the settlement of Jewish farmers and artisans in Israel.

The Birth of Zionism

Into this atmosphere of social degradation and outright persecution came the founder of modern Zionism, Theodor Herzl. Herzl was born on May 2, 1860, in Budapest, Hungary to a well-to-do middle-class family. He was exposed to anti-Semitism at a young age when he was forced to transfer to a mostly Jewish school because of a prejudiced atmosphere in his chosen school.

In 1878, he and his family moved from Budapest to Vienna where Herzl entered the University of Vienna to study law. He received his license to practice law in 1884, but eventually decided to earn a living as a writer. Over the next several years he became a journalist and a marginally successful playwright.

In 1889, he married the daughter of a wealthy Jewish businessman in Vienna. Although this marriage produced three children, it turned out to be an unhappy one for Herzl and his wife. Their troubled marriage was due partly to the strong attachment that Herzl had with his mother and partly because his wife did not share the same zeal for Zionism as Herzl would grow to have.

Herzl's zionistic efforts did not begin in earnest until the last decade of the nineteenth century. Up until that point in his life, Herzl believed that the best way for the Jewish race to survive was to learn how to assimilate into their respective cultures. Very soon, however, he observed an incident that changed his views completely.

In 1891, Herzl went to Paris on assignment for the *Neue Freie Presse*, an influential Viennese newspaper. In Paris, Herzl was dismayed to find the same anti-Semitism that pervaded Vienna and Eastern Europe. Herzl had expected better from the people that had produced the French Revolution. He began to feel that assimilation would never produce the desired result for the Jewish people.

In 1894, a Jewish officer in the French Army was unjustly accused of treason. His supposed crime was that he had given French military documents to German agents. This incident, known as the Dreyfus Affair, and the political turmoil it caused sparked a wave of anti-Semitism in France.

Herzl was witness to angry mobs of Frenchmen shouting "Death to the Jews!" Herzl in later years would claim that the Dreyfus Affair had made a Zionist out of him. Theodor Herzl now believed that so long as anti-Semitism existed, assimilation would never be possible. The only answer for the Jews was organized emigration to a land of their own.

Herzl's first effort on behalf of Zionism was to meet with one of the wealthiest men of his time, Baron Maurice de Hirsch. De Hirsch had founded the Jewish Colonization Association, which concentrated on settling Jews in Argentina and other parts of the

Americas. In this meeting Herzl argued that the Jews needed a political organization to unite them under one flag rather than having them depend on philanthropists such as De Hirsch. This meeting obviously did not have much of an effect on De Hirsch, who did not even hear Herzl out. It did have a profound effect on Herzl though. It prompted him to write *Der Judenstaat (The Jewish State,* 1896).

In *The Jewish State,* Herzl espoused the need of a land for the Jewish people. He wrote:

> The idea which I have developed in this pamphlet is a very old one: it is the restoration of the Jewish State.... Everything depends on our propelling force. And what is that force? The misery of the Jews....I am absolutely convinced that I am right, though I doubt whether I shall live to see myself proved to be so. Those who are the first to inaugurate this movement will scarcely live to see its glorious close. But the inauguration of it is enough to give them a feeling of pride and the joy of spiritual freedom.

Herzl continued on, explaining the need for political organization and activism to reach their goal:

> I think the Jewish question is no more a social than a religious one, notwithstanding that it sometimes takes these and other forms. It is a national question, which can only be solved by making it a political world-

question to be discussed and settled by the civilized nations of the world in council.

Herzl's book was to be a rallying point for the Jews of Eastern Europe. In June 1896, Herzl boarded a train bound for Istanbul to meet with the Ottoman Sultan. He wanted to obtain a land grant, to what was then called Palestine, from the Turkish leader. When the train stopped in Sofia, Bulgaria, hundreds of Jews were there to greet Herzl and cheer him on.

It was in Bulgaria that the Jewish people began to accept him as the leader of the Zionist movement. When Herzl finally got to Istanbul, he waited for eleven days but failed to reach the Sultan. Even though he failed in his attempt, he began his career as the organizer and driving force behind the Jewish goal of establishing a homeland. He continued in this position until his death just eight years later.

Herzl next went to London in an effort to gain support for a Jewish state. His presence there was opposed by the Jewish leaders because of his unpopular political views. As much as he was rejected by the leaders though, he was embraced by the Jewish masses. Herzl was a tall, striking figure with a flowing beard and the bearing of a prophet. His forceful charisma swayed the people but was ineffective against the Jewish leaders, so he left London to find a better way to motivate the Jews.

The First Zionist Congress

Herzl decided to organize a congress of Zionists in 1897 with the prospect of uniting the masses of Jewish people for his cause. This congress was first going to meet in Munich, Germany but was moved to Basel, Switzerland after the heavily assimilated Jewish leaders of Munich opposed it. The congress met at the end of August in 1897. Almost 200 Jews of varying nationalities and social status attended the congress. There were Orthodox religious Jews and atheists, businessmen and students; all were represented at the meeting. Several interested non-participants were also watching, including some Christians and members of the Press. As Theodor Herzl greeted those gathered for this historic event, they roared their support.

"We want to lay the foundation stone," he declared, "of the house which is to shelter the Jewish nation….Zionism is a return to the Jewish fold even before it is a return to the Jewish land." The three-day congress produced an agenda that became known as the Basel Program, which stated "Zionism seeks to obtain for the Jewish people a publicly recognized, legally secured homeland in Palestine." This assembly, the First Zionist Congress, also succeeded in founding the Zionist Organization with Theodor Herzl as President.

Immediately after the First Zionist Congress, Herzl began to publish the Zionist weekly *Die Welt*. He also renewed his efforts to obtain a land settlement for the Jewish people in Israel. Herzl again went to visit the Sultan in Turkey, but was unsuccessful in negotiating a program that would allow mass settlement for the Jews. He decided to pursue his goal in Great Britain. He felt that there was favorable sentiment in England for the establishment of a settlement in the Sinai Peninsula, but he could not convince them to finally surrender the land.

Great Britain did, however, offer an area of land in Uganda, Africa, where they would allow the Jews autonomous control. Herzl, who viewed this option as a temporary solution for Jews in immediate danger, announced this offer at the Sixth Zionist Congress in 1903 and it sparked an instant controversy. In fact, the opposition to the Uganda Program almost split the fledgling Zionist movement in two.

Amidst the controversy over the Uganda Program, Theodor Herzl developed a heart ailment. His steadfast dedication to creating a Jewish homeland in Israel had taken a toll on his physical condition, and he died in 1904. In 1905, the Zionist Congress formally rejected the Uganda Program.

Although Herzl did not live to see his dream come to fruition, his efforts provided the essential framework for the birth of the state of Israel. After the First Zionist Congress in Basel, Herzl had written in his diary:

> If I were to sum up the Basel Congress in a single phrase I would say: In Basel I created the Jewish State. Were I to say this aloud I would be greeted by universal laughter. But perhaps five years hence, in any case, certainly fifty years hence, everyone will perceive it.

Theodor Herzl was buried in Vienna but, as were his wishes, his remains were transferred to Jerusalem in 1949 after the creation of the Jewish state. His grave is on a hill west of the city, a hill known as Mount Herzl.

A Return To Israel

Herzl's actions paved the way for the return of the Jews to Israel. Although God allowed several different events to take place in history that contributed to the return of the Jews, the main event that caused the Jews to immigrate to their ancient homeland was World War II. If Theodor Herzl provided the infrastructure for Zionism's ultimate goal, then World War II was the catalyst that finally created the state.

Although persecution was not new to the Jews, it reached its most horrendous level during the Holocaust. Jewish immigration to Israel during the first half of the twentieth century was sporadic. Before 1933 and the rise of the Third Reich, most immigration was motivated by "pogroms" (organized persecution) in Russia and other parts of Eastern Europe. In the period between 1929 and 1939, immigration to Israel exploded.

The population of Jewish people in Israel ballooned to 450,000 people. The Nazi's accession to power caused increased aliya from Germany. The fear of Nazi aggression also caused more and more Jews from Eastern Europe to make aliya to Israel. Many of these Jews from Germany were professionals and they contributed greatly to the growing Jewish presence in the land.

The port in Haifa as well as oil refineries and other industrial endeavors were undertaken and completed at this time. The Jewish people were gaining a foothold in the land that would result in a declaration of independence for the state of Israel just a decade later. During World War II, aliya took on a more desperate tone.

The British, who were in control of Israel at the time, allowed only 18,000 legal immigrants per year, so the vast majority of immigration during this era was illegal. Sixty-six ships sailing with illegal immigrants on board tried to break the British blockade during these years, but very few actually made it. Many were even sent back to Europe where they faced certain persecution at the hands of the Nazi regime. Even through such opposition, Jewish immigration continued and the Jewish population at the time of the statehood of Israel was around 650,000.

The end of World War II brought to light the devastation of the Holocaust. With the surrender of the Nazi powers to the Allied forces came the realization that the world had stood by and let millions of Jews die. The pressure was on to somehow amend the situation and the Zionist Organization offered one convenient solution: the creation of a homeland for the Jewish survivors of the Holocaust.

Israel's Statehood

The years between the war's end and Israel's statehood were marked by the dogged determination of the battered Jewish population to create a state. Again, boatloads of immigrants defied British rule by landing on the shores of Israel with the intent of forging a new life. Thousands also entered by foot through Syria.

Underground Jewish fighting forces united in a systematic struggle against British authority. These forces protected Jewish neighborhoods and schools and aided in helping thousands of European Jews to settle in their new homeland. Future Prime Minister Menachem Begin was the leader of one of these fierce fighting groups.

The Zionist Organization also played a crucial role at this time. Jewish support was coordinated around the world and a vast network was set up to lobby for the creation of a Jewish state. The United States proved to be an invaluable ally to the cause. In October 1946 President Harry Truman announced his support of the Jewish Agency's plan to partition Israel into separate Jewish and Arab states. In November 1947 Resolution 181, guaranteeing the partition of Israel, was adopted by the United Nations' General Assembly. Finally, on May 14, 1948, David Ben-Gurion boldly announced the creation of the state of Israel.

Within hours of the declaration of statehood, five Arab armies, and units from several other Arab countries, attacked the infant state and plunged it into the War of Independence. Israel suffered 6,000 fatalities (one percent of its population at the time) but eventually emerged victorious from this war. The young country declared a "right of return" to every Jew throughout the world. This brought about two major waves of immigration.

The first was from the Holocaust-scarred countries of Europe. A large number of immigrants arrived from Poland, Hungary, and other Eastern and Western European countries. The second wave of immigration involved mostly Jews from Arab countries in both the Middle East and North Africa. The absorption of these hundreds of thousands of immigrants was extremely difficult, but the young country met the challenge with vigor.

Temporary dwellings were erected and later replaced with permanent ones. Schools were built in which the revived Hebrew language was taught. Employment opportunities were created as Israel sought to provide the chance for a democratic society free of persecution for the Jewish people.

God's hand at work behind the scenes in the creation of the state of Israel bespeaks the miracle our generation has been allowed to witness. But the miracle is two-fold, for with the establishment of the state came the aliya, the immigration of the Jewish people from around the world to their ancient homeland. However, this was just the beginning.

Chapter 6
Aliya from the North

Our church gathered together around the tables for a Passover Seder in Jerusalem. At the table were Jews who were following the command that God gave Moses over thirty-five hundred years ago to partake of the Passover Seder on a yearly basis. During the Seder, a family sits down and rehearses the Exodus out of Egypt. The little children learn how to pass the story of the Passover down to future generations. The Seder includes a special meal consisting of at least three ingredients: lamb, bitter herbs, and unleavened bread.

This particular Passover Seder, sponsored by our church in Jerusalem, was being used as an evangelistic tool to reach out to Jews and show them that Jesus Christ is the "Passover lamb." The majority of those visiting this particular Passover Seder were new Jewish immigrants from the former Soviet Union, most of them coming from Russia.

As I sat there, enjoying the meal and listening to the Exodus story being read by our pastor, Meno Kalisher, I caught myself looking into the faces of the new Russian immigrants. For the very first time since they had moved to the land of Israel, these Jews were taking part in a Passover Seder. I was reminded that the Prophet Jeremiah had said there would be a time, at the time of the end, when Jewish families would talk about an exodus; not the one out of Egypt, but an exodus out of the "north."

Jeremiah's Prophecy

Before looking at the prophecy from the Scriptures

that deals with this subject, notice the prophecy that God gave to Jeremiah for the Jewish people. It is that which will happen at the time of the end. When we talk about the "time of the end" from a Jewish perspective, we're talking about the time during and at the end of the seven-year Tribulation Period. We're talking about a time that follows the Rapture of the Church, when Christians are taken to be with Christ.

After that seven-year Tribulation Period, or as it may be known in the Jewish world "the seventieth week of Daniel," Jesus Christ will return to the earth and establish His kingdom which God has promised to the Jewish people. In Jeremiah 30–33, God gave His prophet a message of solace, to console the Jewish people. The chapters before and after this little section in the Scriptures are messages of judgment upon the Jewish people and upon the neighbors of the Jewish people.

In Jeremiah 31, God talks about resurrecting a people—*the Jewish people*—that had been scattered across the entire world. These people would be placed in a land—*Israel*—that God had promised their forefathers. He talks about resurrecting a language—*the Hebrew language*—that would be given to these people who come from all the nations of the world; with their many different languages they will need one way to communicate with each other.

God is in the process of taking these resurrected people and putting them in a resurrected land. He has given them a resurrected language. The vast majority of these people have a spiritual desire inside. It is on these people that the promise of a new covenant, which will bring all of the Jewish people (the house of Israel) under His Lordship, will be fulfilled. In the future, there is a time when He will put His law in their inward parts and write it on their hearts, and they will be His people and He will be their God.

In addition, God has promised to resurrect their city, the City of Jerusalem, giving it to them once again because of His eternal purpose to dwell among His Jewish people forever. He has chosen Jerusalem. Psalm 132:13 proclaims, *"For the Lord hath chosen Zion."* (The names Zion, City of David, and Jerusalem are synonymous terms for the City of Jerusalem.) Again, *"For the Lord hath chosen [Jerusalem]; he hath desired it for his habitation. This is my rest for ever: here will I dwell; for I have desired it"* (Psalm 132:13-14). These are the desires of God Himself to dwell among His people forever.

An Exodus From The North

In Jeremiah 31:8, God gives the promise of resurrecting a people, *"Behold, I will bring them from the north country, and gather them from the coasts of the earth."* Then in verse 10 He says, *"He that scattered Israel will gather him, and keep him, as a shepherd doth his flock."* But He talks initially about bringing them from the north.

All geographical direction in the Bible is from Jerusalem. In Ezekiel 5:5, God says that He put Jerusalem in the center of the earth and then He placed all the nations around her. The gathering from the "north" is to the north of Jerusalem. In the Book of Jeremiah an interesting prophetic promise is laid out for everyone to read and understand. In fact, this prophecy is unique to the time in which we live.

Jeremiah 16:13 says, *"Therefore will I cast you out of this land into a land that ye know not, neither ye nor your fathers; and there shall ye serve other gods day and night; where I will not show you favour."* God gave Moses this same prophecy in Deuteronomy 28 when

He said if you won't be obedient to Me, and follow My statutes then I will cast you into the four corners of the earth. That is exactly what Jeremiah reiterates when he quotes what God has told him, *"Therefore will I cast you out of this land into a land that ye know not."* Verse 14 says, *"Therefore, behold, the days come, saith the Lord, that it shall no more be said, The Lord liveth, that brought up the children of Israel out of the land of Egypt."* In Exodus 12:14 there is a command that God gives Moses and the Jewish people: once a year, at the time of Passover, they are to rehearse at a Passover Seder the events that took place surrounding the Exodus out of Egypt.

Jeremiah 16:14 reveals that they will not be talking at the Passover table about the exodus out of the land of Egypt. What then will they be talking about? Verse 15 explains, *"But, The Lord liveth, that brought up the children of Israel from the land of the north, and from all the lands whither he had driven them."*

The phrase, "from all the lands," defines the fact that He is not talking about the return out of the Babylonian captivity only, but from all the lands where Jewish people would have been living the last two thousand years. Therefore, Jeremiah is speaking of the time in history when the Jewish people come not only from the "north," but "all the lands" where they have been living.

When the Jews were dispersed in 70 A.D. under General Titus and the Roman Army, they were dispersed to all four corners of the earth, into all the nations of the world. That was more than one hundred and twenty-five nations, and those nations are now represented in Israel by returning Jews making aliya back into the land.

The Prophet Jeremiah, in chapter 16 (verses 13

and 14), tells the Jewish people that they are going to be dispersed, God is going to bring them back into the land of Israel, and they are not going to talk about the exodus out of Egypt. Instead, they'll be talking about the exodus out of the north at a time when God will bring them from all the lands where they have been scattered.

As an example, verse 15 says, *"I will bring them again into their land that I gave unto their fathers."* A promise that God would reach into the north and bring these Jewish people out of that land and into the land He has promised to give them. In Jeremiah 23:7-8, He reiterates this promise, *"Therefore, behold, the days come, saith the Lord, that they shall no more say, The Lord liveth, which brought up the children of Israel out of the land of Egypt; But, The Lord liveth, which brought up and which led the seed of the house of Israel out of the north country, and from all countries whither I had driven them; and they shall dwell in their own land."*

God emphasizes once again that He is going to reach into the north and He is going to bring these people out of the north back into their land. The same thing is spoken of again in Jeremiah 31:8, *"Behold I will bring them from the north country."*

Modern-Day Partial Fulfillment

Since we have moved to Israel, living now in the City of Jerusalem, Judy and I have witnessed the exodus out of the north (from Russia and the former Soviet Union) and the immigration, or aliya, into the land of Israel. Time after time we have been at Ben-Gurion International Airport where we would see the planes arrive from the "north" carrying Jews from the former Soviet Union. As they would off-load the plane, with nervous excitement, these Jewish immigrants began to realize that they were coming "home" for the first time.

Over the years, Jews from the "north" (Russia) have steadily immigrated to Israel. However, since 1989 this immigration has been much more noticeable because of an increase in the number of new immigrants. In the early 1990s the numbers were very high. The latest figures indicate that over 850,000 Jews have made aliya from the north, making their way into Israel.

One reason for these large numbers of immigrants from the former Soviet Union is the fear of the Jews that the Russian government will slam shut the gates of Jewish emigration, which were opened wide after the breakup of the Soviet Union. Such apprehension is based on the chance that the Communist Party's influence on the government could impact the situation. This concern rocks agencies throughout the country that deal with Russian Jews firsthand.

This fear is pretty intense because of the possibility that there will be a slowing down, if not an end to emigration. Threats to emigration have already appeared. The closing of offices of the Jewish Agency, which oversees and encourages Jewish emigration, started under the government of Boris Yeltsin. Meanwhile, many of Russia's Jews have headed to Poland and other Central European nations in case the government forces a swift and dramatic change in emigration policy.

Reports out of Russia say that it's really like the Wild West. They say these people have no idea what's about to happen to them. Russian Jews see the worst-case scenario with an implementation of a militant anti-Western policy, a massive nationalization of private property, and a crackdown on minority rights and emigration. Even the election of Vladamir Putin could lead to petty harassment of international groups as a concession to pressures by ultra-nationalists.

Russian Jews feel that the Yeltsin government was of little help to them and now with Yeltsin's handpicked successor, Putin, they fear what he will do to stop the growth of anti-Semitism and fascism. In 1987, some 250,000 American Jews marched on Washington, D.C., calling on then Soviet President Mikhail Gorbachev to open the gates of the Soviet Union to Jewish emigration. That dramatic expression of solidarity climaxed decades of American Jewish rallying for Soviet Jewish freedom.

But that concern receded as Gorbachev's reform policies of Glasnost gave way to the collapse of communism. Soviet authorities relaxed emigration restrictions, allowing the exodus of hundreds of thousands of Jews. Almost one million have since come to Israel. In addition, 300,000 Soviet Jews have immigrated to the United States. In recent years, some 36,000 Jews have left the former Soviet Union annually.

Now, longtime Jewish experts and activists are watching tensely and waiting to see if the continuing changes of power in the Russian government could throw Russia back to the bad old days of iron-fisted, anti-Jewish Communist rule. Mark Levin, executive director of the National Conference on Soviet Jewry, has said there is serious concern over the prospect of Communist control of the Russian government: "Everything party officials have said about which way the country should be moving makes us anxious about what the future might hold for the Jewish population."

Russian Jews Today

Most statistics show a large number of Jews still live

in Russia. Russian census figures put the number of Jews and their families at roughly 600,000, but the census is unreliable and the actual numbers may be higher. According to a highly–placed Israeli official, about 300,000 Russian Jews hold "invitations" from Israel as "an insurance policy"—just in case. Already there are signs that Russian Jewish emigration may have slowed.

Russian officials, in the past, suspended the license of the Jewish Agency of Israel on charges it was meddling in Russian affairs. This move has been interpreted by some as a nationalist show of force. Under Boris Yeltsin, many of the offices used to process Jewish emigration were closed down. The *Washington Post* reported that the official Interfax News Agency had quoted Russian officials as saying the Jewish Agency is a front for Mossad, Israel's intelligence agency. Jewish Agency officials declined to address such rumors.

While anti-Semitism long has been a problem in Russia, new indications of a resurgence have surfaced. At Communist rallies, anti-Semitic materials have been circulated while swastikas and hangman's nooses have been spray-painted on the walls of Moscow's main synagogue. A synagogue in the city of Yaroslavl has been firebombed. No one has been arrested.

There have been calls for a ban on Jews appearing on Russian television. Victor Anpilov, while leader of the Working Russia Party, told the NTV channel that "most of those who appear on Russian television are people of Jewish descent" and should be banned. Privately, some experts, many of whom are reluctant to use their names, say they are "preparing for the worst."

Because of Russia's economic woes and pressure from nationalists and Communists, the government recently has shifted rightward. The most critical sign is the ever-increasing number of government officials who look like the old-style Soviet *apparatchik*, with strong ties to the Arab world and little deference to the West, according to a report issued by the National Conference on Soviet Jewry and the Anti-Defamation League. Many of this new breed of Russian leaders, especially the Communist leaders, are deeply troubled by what they perceive as the Jewish influence over a West that is hostile to Russia.

They believe that the Western world's culture, thus the Jewish Diaspora, increasingly influences ideology and world-view. They see its influence growing, literally by the hour, not just the day. They say that had Stalin lived longer he would have restored Russia and saved it from the "Cosmopolitans" (the Communist code word for "Jew").

Russian Nationalism

Though there may be a drop in overt anti-Semitism, Russian Jews say there is a lot of nationalism in which all minorities get lumped together as the "other." This nationalism is manifested in the ever-increasing calls for a return to the Russian Empire. One way this can happen is for Russia to deport all non-Russians. Another would be for Russia to expand its borders to the south, which would allow for a warm-water port for Russian naval operations, plus the natural resources needed to give its people a better life.

Jews in Russia today face a different kind of anti-Semitism from that experienced in the past. There used to be state anti-Semitism, keeping Jews from getting certain jobs or being accepted to certain colleges. But despite that, they were safe on the streets. Now, however, anti-Semitism has shifted, moving from high governmental authority down into the streets.

Organized and petty crime is at an all-time high, and people are no longer safe. Russian experts say that while there are incidents of anti-Semitism, the rising fear comes from widespread anarchy and violence.

Despite anti-Semitism, there are mixed feelings about Jewish emigration. On the one hand, Russia doesn't want people to leave who are talented and smart. On the other, when the scapegoats leave, who is there to blame if things go wrong? This is a very twisted mentality. The Jewish world's work in the region remains unfinished. The issue of emigration from the former Soviet Union is far from over. The scale may be smaller, but the challenge remains.

Today many Jews still remain in the area formerly know as the Soviet Union. For the last several years there has been concern about the potential for these Jews to emigrate and go to Israel. Two problems stand in their way: emigration procedures in Russia and the rise in anti-Semitism and nationalism in that area. The Israeli government and private organizations have been working to eliminate these roadblocks so that another wave of "aliya from the north" can begin.

Chapter 7
Aliya from Ethiopia

It was Friday afternoon in Jerusalem, just before the beginning of Shabbat. Most of the businesses had closed and families were getting ready for the Jewish Sabbath day of rest, which would begin at sundown. On this lazy afternoon I thought I might check out the latest world news and tuned my radio to the British Broadcasting Corporation's international broadcast. As journalists worldwide do, I monitor other news gathering organizations. Tuning in the BBC, I heard them mention that "Operation Solomon" was about to get under way.

Immediately this caught my attention and I was eager to find out what Operation Solomon was all about. Not being familiar with the code name, I contacted some of my unnamed sources to get more information. ("Unnamed sources" is a term used to describe people who feed us information, and we do not tell who they are.)

Having gathered the information about Operation Solomon, I immediately got on the telephone to the network that I represented, as a stringer, in Israel. (A stringer is a free-lance news correspondent.) I made contact with a network operating out of Washington, D.C., and announced that Operation Solomon was under way. I later found out that I had scooped—by two-and-a-half hours—ABC, NBC, CBS, and CNN with my report on the beginning of Operation Solomon.

Operation Solomon was a massive logistical undertaking that is a testimony to the level of Israel's commitment in protecting world Jewry. The Israeli government is dedicated to bringing Jews back under the safety net of Israel, and as soon as possible. This was the case with Operation Solomon. Jews from modern-day Ethiopia were to be airlifted from their homeland to the safety of Israel, their spiritual homeland, in a matter of hours, not days. The Bible speaks of Ethiopian Jews returning to the land, so for us as Christians, what seems to be this modern-day fulfillment of ancient Biblical prophecy is nothing short of thrilling!

Ethiopian Jewish History

The story of the Ethiopian Jews begins roughly three thousand years ago. It was then that a Jewish population began to flourish in what is now modern-day Ethiopia. There are varied accounts as to their origins. Some say that they are the descendants of Menelik I, son of King Solomon and Queen Sheba, while others say they could be the lost tribe of Dan. In fact, there is another theory which says they are the remnants of Jews who fled Israel at the time of the destruction of the First Temple in 586 B.C. and settled in Ethiopia. Whatever the case, these people claimed the name Beta Israel (House of Israel) and have followed the Torah for centuries.

At their largest, Beta Israel's population numbered almost a half million strong. They were powerful enough to resist the waves of Moslem attacks, which were waged against them throughout the centuries. Beta Israel lived in relative security until the Solomonic Empire of the thirteenth century began to increase the religious intolerance in Ethiopia.

This "religious cleansing" continued until it reached its culmination in 1624 with the final defeat of Beta Israel. The Ethiopian Jews then suffered much like the

Jewish Zealots in Israel in the first century. They were made to work as slaves and all their religious writings were burned.

This persecution decreased over the years, but never subsided. Beta Israel struggled along with a meager existence. The population dropped from 500,000 to less than 100,000. Then, in 1973, things again took a turn for the worse for the Ethiopian Jews when Colonel Mengistu Haile Mariam assumed control of the Ethiopian government. Mengistu was a Marxist-Leninist dictator who rose to power by way of a military coup. In what was to be a portent of things to come, 2,500 Jews were killed and over 7,000 were rendered homeless in Mengistu's first week in power.

Beta Israel's population suffered greatly over the next few years. Mengistu began to relocate the Jews into state-run villages. This had the effect of producing widespread anti-Semitism among established villagers. The Colonel forbade the practice of Judaism in the early 1980s and began imprisoning many Jews for being "Zionist spies." Mengistu also instituted forced conscription for Jewish boys at the age of twelve. Many of these boys were taken from their parents never to see them again. Finally, all this persecution was piled on top of what were already horrendous living conditions in poverty-stricken Ethiopia.

In Israel at this time, Menachem Begin had just become Prime Minister. Begin was a passionate man who felt a strong duty to protect Jews around the world. He began a practice of selling arms to Mengistu in the hopes that he could curry favor with him. After one of these arms shipments, Begin asked Mengistu if he could bring back 200 Jews on the now empty cargo plane. Mengistu relented. This small airlift was a precursor of larger operations in the future. Over the next several years, small numbers of Jews were able to sneak out of Ethiopia and make their way to Israel.

Operation Moses

Beta Israel's first mass exodus to Israel came in 1984. This airlift, under the code name "Operation Moses," transferred 8,000 Ethiopian Jews from neighboring Sudan to Israel. Most of these immigrants were young men because they were the only ones who could make the arduous trek to Sudan. Unfortunately, women, children, and elderly were left behind almost exclusively. This operation was able to rescue only about one-third of Beta Israel because when the Arab nations learned what was going on, they pressured Sudan into stopping the flights.

In an interesting gesture, then U.S. Vice President George Bush was able to organize the CIA into sponsoring another small operation, which was known as "Operation Joshua." This operation, staged shortly after Operation Moses, rescued 800 more Ethiopian Jews. Although these airlifts helped, Mengistu suddenly cracked down on emigration and things again began to look bleak for Beta Israel. Zionist organizations continued to work on their behalf, but Mengistu was steadfast in his stance. He allowed a small trickle of people to leave when food shortages in Ethiopia forced him to accept humanitarian aid from Israel and the United States.

Israel's continued efforts on behalf of Beta Israel paid off in the form of an agreement with Ethiopia in 1990. This agreement allowed Ethiopian Jews who had family in Israel to reunite with them. This family reunification rule was quickly expanded and emigration began to rise. Beta Israel was beginning to see the fulfillment of prophecy foretold in the Books of Zephaniah and Isaiah more than twenty-six hundred years ago.

The Jewish emigration from Ethiopia was progressing fairly well; however, quite a few Jews remained stranded in Ethiopia. Suddenly, in early 1991, events took a dramatic turn when rebel forces began to make advances on the capital city of Addis Ababa. The rebel attacks became so effective that they caused Mengistu to flee Ethiopia in early May. Rebels took control of the city and the whole country fell into chaos.

The Top Priority

In Israel, the Ethiopian Jews became the top priority. The situation was very pressing because at any moment the rebels could take these Jewish hostages and use them as bargaining chips with the United States or Israel. The government, headed by Prime Minister Yitzhak Shamir, sprang into action and initiated Operation Solomon. They issued a special permit for the Israeli National Airline, El Al, allowing them to fly on the Sabbath.

On Friday, May 24, 1991, thirty-four El Al 747s and Hercules C-130s took off from Ben-Gurion International Airport and made their way across the southern portion of Israel, flying over the Red Sea, over the Sinai Peninsula, and finally into an area of Africa that would take them into Addis Ababa, Ethiopia.

These planes, with seats taken out so as many Ethiopian Jews as possible could be taken on board, operated continuously for thirty-six hours. In fact, one of the 747s, which normally carried 500 passengers, counted 1,087 people on the plane as it made its way to Israel. While that particular plane was in the air, between Addis Ababa and Jerusalem, seven babies were born during the flight. When it was all over, Operation Solomon had rescued an incredible 14,324 Jews from Ethiopia and brought them to Israel.

That Saturday when they arrived in Israel, they were taken to absorption centers in Jerusalem and Tel Aviv. These absorption centers help new immigrants assimilate into Israeli society. One of these centers was located near our church, so after our services Judy and I decided to go there in hopes of interviewing some of these newly arrived Ethiopian Jews. When we arrived at the absorption center in Jerusalem, we saw many of the immigrants barefoot and dressed in their native attire. There were young mothers with their babies still strapped to their backs. Some of the elderly looked as if they were in a trance, amazed at what had happened in the last forty-eight hours.

I was not able to interview any of the new immigrants because they could not speak English, but I was able to do an actuality. In an actuality, a journalist presents a report with the noise of the event in the background. This was an amazing story that had to be told, not only for the humanitarian side of the story, but from the prophetic significance of all that was related to the events surrounding the Ethiopian Jews.

When it came time for lunch, we followed the immigrants into the cafeteria. Plates filled with Israeli cuisine were placed in front of the exhausted travelers. Each plate held yogurt, tomatoes, cucumbers, olives, a boiled egg, and pickles. At first the Ethiopians just stared at the plates not knowing what to do. They had been used to eating a "mush-like" food with pita bread, so they didn't even know how to go about eating the food that was set before them.

I went up to an elderly man, cracked his boiled egg for him, and showed him how to eat it. I continued to another table where a woman sat with her baby. I opened up their container of yogurt and started to spoon feed the hungry child. As I went from table to table, helping these starving people, tears started running down my cheeks. I was reminded of a prophecy related to these people. These Ethiopian Jews had returned "home" after almost two thousand years.

Zephaniah's Prophecy

The Prophet Zephaniah wrote that in the time of the end, the time right before Jesus Christ returns to the earth, there would be an aliya out of Ethiopia. Zephaniah 3:10 says, *"From beyond the rivers of Ethiopia my suppliants, even the daughter of my dispersed, shall bring mine offering."* (The word "suppliants" refers to a multitude of worshipers, as in Isaiah 66:20.)

The prophecy states that the children of those who had been living outside the land of Israel will return to Israel as a multitude of worshipers. They will be brought back as an offering to God. Isaiah speaks of the *"brethren...an offering unto the Lord"* (Isaiah 66:20). Isaiah also reveals that the Ethiopians will return upon horses or whatever vehicles can be used to return the Ethiopians to Israel.

In 1991, the Israelis used thirty-four airplanes to bring starving Ethiopian Jews back to Israel. Isaiah refers to a period of time that will be the ultimate aliya out of Ethiopia, to take place during that seven-year period of time leading up to the return of the Messiah at the Second Coming. What we saw in May 1991 was but a foretaste of that which will take place in the future: Aliya from Ethiopia.

TREND 2
Alignment

Chapter 8
Alignment of the Nations

Living in Jerusalem as a journalist and being a student of Biblical prophecy, I pay close attention to Israel's neighbors. The more I observe them, the more I sense that their military activities are coming together as predicted by the ancient Jewish prophets.

I have watched closely the military maneuvers undertaken by an elite commando unit of the Syrian Army, stationed at the northern border of Israel. I have observed the military exercises of Egypt in the Sinai desert, at the southern border of Israel. I have reported on terrorists who cross the Jordan River coming from the Hashemite Kingdom of Jordan. For thirty-nine Scud attacks, I sat in a sealed room anticipating a fatal blow from a nuclear or biological warhead coming from Iraq's Saddam Hussein to Israel.

All of these activities, coupled with my studies of Biblical prophecy, have helped me to realize that the nations of the world are aligning themselves against the Jewish people. Alignment is the second trend that gives us evidence of the possible soon coming of the Messiah.

Before we start talking about how these and other nations are aligning themselves against Israel, we must first find out about the origins of the nations. We must understand what unfolded in the first two thousand years of human history. That history will help us as we seek to understand the thought processes of the countries that will come against Israel.

In The Beginning

A proper view of history takes us back to the book of beginnings, the Book of Genesis. We begin our study of human history with an overview of the first twelve chapters of Genesis.

Genesis Chapter 1 *is the story of creation.*

Genesis Chapter 2 *is the special effects of creation.*

Genesis Chapter 3 *is the narrative of the fall of Adam and Eve; the fall of man.*

Genesis Chapter 4 *is the story of Cain and Abel.*

Genesis Chapter 5 *is a chapter of genealogies; from Adam, the first man, to Noah, who would face the Flood.*

Genesis Chapters 6, 7 and 8 *are the story of the Flood.*

Genesis Chapter 9 *is the story of Noah after the Flood.*

Genesis Chapter 10 *is another genealogy; from Noah and his three sons (Shem, Ham, and Japheth), into the beginnings of the repopulation of the earth after the Flood.*

Genesis Chapter 11 *is the story of the Tower of Babel and the breaking down of obedience to God's command to be fruitful, multiply, and replenish the earth.*

Genesis Chapter 12 *is the story of Abraham coming out of Ur of the Chaldees into the Promised Land and establishing the nation of the Jewish people on the land that God promised to give His chosen people.*

This overview of the first twelve chapters of Genesis is critical to an understanding of how God is going to align the nations in the last days. These summaries create a backdrop for a proper study of the nations.

From Creation To Nations

Beginning in Genesis 1, we find the first command that God gave to man; a command given to the first people on earth, Adam and Eve. After creating man and woman in verse 27, He goes on to say in verse 28, *"God blessed them, and God said unto them, Be fruitful, and multiply, and [fill] the earth."* God's command to Adam and Eve—the very first command recorded in the Bible—was to be fruitful and multiply and to fill the earth.

For the next fifteen hundred years, that is exactly what took place. In the genealogy of Genesis 5, we see the record of what happened, and that people were being multiplied on the earth. Some scholars have estimated that the earth's population at the time of the Flood was approximately one billion people. Adam and Eve had been obedient to God; they were filling the earth with people.

However, because sin entered into the world through Adam and Eve, mankind became more sinful as time went by. As mankind increased in evil deeds, God realized that He must put a stop to all this depravity. God came to a place where He determined He had to rid the world of this evil element and start over again with just a handful of righteous people.

The Flood was the judgment that God brought upon these people that He had created. These were people who had evil desires and goals and wanted to come against His will on this earth. After the Flood took place, only eight people were left on the earth. Noah and his three sons, Shem, Ham, and Japheth, and their four wives were the only survivors of the Flood.

It is interesting to note that the first statement God made after the Flood was a command. It was a similar command to the one He gave to Adam and Eve. Genesis 9:1 says, *"And God blessed Noah and his sons, and said unto them, Be fruitful, and multiply, and replenish the earth."* The command that God gave to Noah and his family was to be fruitful and multiply and to replenish the earth, to repopulate the earth with people that God wants to have to worship Him and love Him.

A Record Of Obedience

Just as Genesis 5 is a genealogy from Adam to Noah, Genesis 10 is a genealogy from Noah into the future, and it states that the command to repopulate the earth was being obeyed. Genesis 10:1 says, *"These are the generations of the sons of Noah...and unto them were sons born after the flood."* As we consider this, we begin to see the alignment of the nations that will come together in the end times against the Jewish people.

In Genesis 10:2, the sons of Japheth are listed. These include: Gomer, Magog, Tubal, and Meshech. In verse 3, Gomer's son Togarmah is named. Ezekiel talks about a coalition of nations that will come against Israel at the time of the end. In Ezekiel 38, the prophet names the nations who will come against Israel and the list includes: Magog, Tubal, Meshech, Gomer, and Togarmah. As previously seen in Genesis, these are the sons of Japheth.

In Genesis 10:6, the sons of Ham are listed, including: Cush, Mizraim, and Put. Through studying this genealogy, we can see the Arab nations that have developed from Ham, the son of Noah: Cush is modern-day Ethiopia and/or Sudan; Mizraim, is modern-day Egypt; and Put, is modern-day Libya.

Nimrod's Babel

In Genesis 10:8, we see that Noah's grandson Cush (son of Ham) begat Nimrod and Nimrod became a mighty one on the earth. Verse 10 says that the beginning of his kingdom was Babel. Babel became what we know as Babylon, both the Biblical Babylon as well as modern-day Babylon, located in Iraq. Nimrod left the area where Noah's ark rested after the Flood, probably in the area of eastern Turkey on the Mountains of Ararat, and journeyed to Babel to establish his kingdom.

Babel is located on the Euphrates River, approximately sixty miles north of where the Tigris River and the Euphrates River come together to flow into the Persian Gulf. Nimrod, who was a mighty hunter before the Lord, began his kingdom in Babel. Genesis 10:10 states this fact more plainly when it names the land of Shinar, modern-day Iraq, as the beginning of Nimrod's kingdom.

Are Jews And Arabs Cousins?

Sometimes we get into trouble when we listen to the wrong sources for our understanding of Biblical prophecy. There are prophecy teachers on national television who are propagating a false teaching. I am speaking of news commentators, on all of the major networks, who make statements that contradict God's Word.

We hear reporters claim that they cannot understand the problem in the Middle East between the

Israelis and their Arab neighbors. They say that the Israelis and Arabs are all sons of Father Abraham and then they ask, "So why is there such trouble, why is there a problem today?" If you will notice, I have not yet mentioned the birth of Abraham. Abraham is first mentioned in chapter 11 of the Book of Genesis; we are still in the genealogies of chapter 10.

I have read through the genealogies and I have introduced to you Egypt, which is an Arab country; Iraq, which is an Arab country; Sudan, which is an Arab country; and Libya, which is an Arab country. Abraham is not even on the scene yet. As students of the Bible, we can refute that statement which has been propagated upon us by the media: "There should be no problem since they are all children of Abraham." It is based on a false assertion and it is not a true statement.

In addition to this information, as we look at other Arab states, we find that two-thirds of what we know as modern-day Jordan did not come from Abraham. The narrative of Lot and his family proves this. They were living in Sodom and Gomorrah when God determined He was going to judge the people of those cities. He sent angels to help them escape; and as they were leaving, Lot's wife looked back and was turned into a pillar of salt.

To continue this story, found in Genesis 19:32, Lot's two daughters came up with an evil plan. They said, *"Come, let us make our father drink wine, and we will lie with him, that we may preserve seed of our father."* So, Lot drank wine with his daughters, became drunk, and had sexual relations with both of them.

Genesis 19:36-37 says, *"Thus were both the daughters of Lot with child by their father. And the firstborn bare a son, and called his name Moab,"* and he became the father of the Moabites. The

Moabites inhabit the central third of what we know as modern-day Jordan. Genesis 19:38 says, *"And the younger, she also bare a son, and called his name Ben-ammi,"* the same as the name of the father of the children of Ammon. The Ammonites occupy the northern third of modern-day Jordan.

Jordan is Biblically divided into three parts: Ammon in the north, Moab in the middle, and Edom in the south. Two-thirds of modern-day Jordan did not come from Abraham. The upper two-thirds came from Lot because of the incestuous relationship with his daughters.

Nimrod's Disobedience

Much of the Arab world, then, did not come from Abraham. But let's take a look at the story of how the nations were established. Nimrod found a spot on the Euphrates River in what we know as modern-day Iraq and decided to build a great city. Genesis 11:1-4 says, *"The whole earth was of one language, and of one speech. And it came to pass, as they journeyed from the east, that they found a plain in the land of Shinar; and they dwelt there.*

"And they said one to another, Go to, let us make brick, and burn them thoroughly. And they had brick for stone, and slime had they for mortar. And they said, Go to, let us build us a city and a tower, whose top may reach unto heaven; and let us make us a name, lest we be scattered abroad upon the face of the whole earth."

Remember, God gave a command to Noah and his three sons to be fruitful and multiply and replenish the earth. Instead of following the command that God gave to Nimrod, his father, his grandfather, and his great-grandfather, instead of spreading out across the world and multiplying and replenishing the earth, Nimrod decided to develop one major city. He made Babel a great city, gave it a great name, and then built a tower as a monument to the great people in the city.

One of my early Sunday School teachers taught that the problem in Babel was that God feared Nimrod would build a tower that would reach all the way into Heaven. Nimrod's people made that statement in Genesis 11:4, but they did not really believe that they could build a tower that could reach all the way into Heaven.

God was not having an anxiety attack, believing that a tower was going to reach all the way up into Heaven. God was not afraid that they would have another way of access to the heavenlies other than the plan that He had given them. But even though God was not having an anxiety attack, He was concerned that they were not being obedient to His command to be fruitful, multiply, and replenish the earth.

God's Intervention

After God observed what was going on and He realized that nothing could restrain them from what they had imagined to do, He decided to come down to Babel and confound their language so that they would not be able to understand one another's speech. It would have been very interesting to be an observer at this particular time, when God went down and gave the different languages to those gathered.

It was probably a work day; and Nimrod was probably laboring on a project, trying to build this tower to show the greatness of Babel. All of a sudden everyone started speaking different languages; even Nimrod himself started speaking a different language. The workers couldn't understand the commands that

Nimrod was giving them, so they couldn't work on the tower anymore. In essence, Genesis 11:8 tells us, this is how *"the Lord scattered them abroad from thence upon the face of all the earth."* They left off from building the city and they are going now to do what God told them to do.

Do you ever stop to wonder how God made the decision as to how many people would speak what language? God has used language to divide people into the different nations of the world. In reality, the people of the world are not divided by borders lined in the sand, but instead they are divided by "language borders." You know, most French-speaking people live in France, most Polish-speaking people live in Poland, most German-speaking people live in Germany, and we could go on and on.

The Jewish Factor

I say this tongue-in-cheek, but it does have a true meaning to it. The point I am trying to bring out is that the language barriers or language borders are truly what the boundaries of the nations are today. But how did God make a decision on how many were going to speak what language and how He would divide them? Deuteronomy 32:8 tells us how that all came together, *"When the Most High divided to the nations their inheritance, when he separated the sons of Adam, he set the bounds of the people according to the number of the children of Israel."*

Remember, when God performed this division in Babel (Genesis 11), Abraham was not present yet and the Jewish people were not established. For the first two thousand years of human history, there were only Gentiles upon the face of the earth. In fact, originally a Gentile, Abraham became the father of the Jewish people. (That all takes place in chapter 12 of Genesis.) God divides the people of the world into their different nations or language groups by His foreknowledge of how many Jews would be on the face of the earth, because He had a special purpose.

How did He decide how this all was going to take place? In Deuteronomy 7:6, He says, *"Thou art an holy people unto the Lord thy God: the Lord thy God hath chosen thee."* He's now speaking through Moses to the Jewish people. God chose the Jewish people to be a special people unto Him, above all people that are upon the face of the earth. God made this decision. There are no people who can decide to say to God that they are the chosen. God is choosing whom He wants.

Deuteronomy 7:7 says, *"The Lord did not set his love upon you, nor choose you, because ye were more in number than any people; for ye were the fewest of all people."* It wasn't God's decision to divide the people of the world into their different language groups because the Jewish people were the greatest in number. We know that for sure, because they were the fewest in number. This is the reason He chose the Jewish people, as told in verse 8: *"Because the Lord loved you."*

You could write over the first phrase of verse 8 the word "grace." They did not merit this honor. He knew exactly how they would act. The Jewish people would be a hardheaded, stiff-necked, and hardhearted people. They would not be obedient. He would have to chastise them and He would have to send them into dispersion.

He would have to take them out of the land that He had given them. He would have to bring them under His leadership. But He chose them because He loved them, and that's how He made a decision to give the language groups their locations on the face of the earth and how He divided the nations that would in the end times align themselves against the Jewish people.

National Judgment

If you study God's Word, and in particular the books of the prophets, you'll find out that much is said about nations that will come into some kind of coalition or alignment at the time of the end; alignment against the Jewish people. Much of the Book of Jeremiah deals with these nations coming together. In fact, chapters 46 through 51 give detailed prophecies and pronounce judgment upon nations who are going to come against Israel, not only at the time of the end but throughout the history of the Jewish people.

The Book of Daniel, another prophecy written by one of the ancient Jewish prophets, speaks of nations and empires that come to power and focus their aggressive acts on the Jewish people. In chapters 2 and 7, Daniel gives the prophecy of the Gentile world empires that will come to power. The Babylonian Empire, the first to come on the scene, takes the Jewish people into captivity for seventy years. The Medo-Persian Empire, following on the heels of the Babylonians, came to power under the leadership of Cyrus, a man named by the Prophet Isaiah, one hundred and fifty years earlier, to allow the Jews to return to Jerusalem to rebuild their temple.

The Medes and the Persians were defeated by the Grecian Empire under the leadership of Alexander the Great. At the death of this young world ruler, the empire is divided into four parts, as prophesied by Daniel, two hundred years before it happened. Finally, the Roman Empire, which would be the last great empire until the Revived Roman Empire, defeats all remnants of the previous empires and sets up the most powerful of those four Gentile world powers.

The Revived Roman Empire, which in the end times will come out of the ashes of the Old Roman Empire, will move against the Jewish people. It is out of the Revived Roman Empire that this one-world ruler, the Antichrist, will emerge. This "Superman of the Tribulation" will at first confirm a peace treaty with Israel, and then lead the forces of evil in a fight-to-the-finish battle against the Jewish nation.

It is during the first part of the Tribulation Period, the first three-and-a-half years, when the Antichrist is supposedly protecting Israel that the Prophet Daniel refers to (Daniel 11:40-44). God gave Daniel a prophecy about the "king of the north," which will later be identified as Syria, and the "king of the south," which will be identified as Egypt. These two nations will form a coalition to come against the Jewish people.

The alignment of nations will come in the last days against the Jewish people. The Prophet Ezekiel, in chapter 38, mentions some of the nations we have seen in Genesis 10, including: Magog, Meshech, Tubal, Gomer, Togarmah, Persia, Ethiopia, and Libya. All of these nations will come together to form a coalition against Israel, an alignment of the nations in the last days against Israel. This alignment must happen because the ancient Jewish prophets—through divine inspiration—wrote about it. It will come to pass.

Chapter 9
The Damascus Declaration

As a credentialed journalist stationed in Jerusalem, I reported my perspective on the Gulf Crisis in 1991. All international journalists gathered daily at the Hilton Hotel, which had been set up as a press center. There, we could meet with representatives from the Government Press Office, the Israeli Defense Force, the foreign ministry, and the Prime Minister's office. They all had their media spokespersons headquartered at this press center. The Israeli spokesperson for each agency was always close at hand to give the reporters the latest information.

When a Scud alarm would sound, all of the journalists at this press center would quickly head for the sealed room with our gas masks. We would wait in the sealed room with our gas masks on, waiting for the siren to sound the all-clear signal. Several times during this period, the then spokesperson for the Foreign Minister, and later Prime Minister of Israel, Benjamin Netanyahu, was on CNN being questioned, when a siren sounded the warning of an incoming Scud. It was then that the world would witness the Israelis putting on their gas masks and heading for the sealed room.

As the Gulf Crisis progressed we had opportunities to question U.S. Secretary of State James Baker, who frequently traveled to Jerusalem for the purpose of keeping Israel from retaliating against the attacks by Iraq. Lawrence Eagleberger, who replaced James Baker as Secretary of State, also made many trips to Israel to keep them in line.

It was always interesting to note that when these

men were visiting Israel, they would also be involved in "shuttle diplomacy." After their visit to Israel they would "shuttle" to Damascus to meet with President Assad, the leader of Syria. Then they would "shuttle" down to Cairo to meet with Egyptian President Mubarak.

Either before or after each of these visits by the United States to Syria and Egypt, Assad and Mubarak would get together to discuss how they were going to respond to the pressure that the United States was putting on them to keep their countries from joining Iraq's coalition. It was during these meetings that President Assad and President Mubarak formed somewhat of a coalition. At the conclusion of the crisis, this coalition between Egypt and Syria was reduced to paper and became known as the Damascus Declaration.

The Damascus Declaration

The Damascus Declaration was a treaty signed at the end of the Gulf War. It was designed to promote solidarity among the Arab states that had just recently aligned themselves with the Gulf Cooperation Council. Much of the rhetoric in the Declaration itself seems to be directed at the country of Israel. Although Israel is only mentioned by name a few times, it seems that almost all the Articles could be used in an argument against Israel.

For example, the main reason for the Gulf Cooperation Alliance, headed by the United States, was the supposed "liberation" of Kuwait in the Gulf War. The Damascus Declaration endeavors to draw a parallel to Iraq's invasion of Kuwait and Israel's "occupation" of the Palestinian people. The Declaration is very much a political statement that attempts to show how unified the Arab nations are in their stance against Israel.

The Damascus Declaration could also be seen as being rather hypocritical. The Declaration states that "its member nations are committed to respecting and upholding historical and brotherly ties and good neighborly relations; an obligation to respect the territorial integrity, regional safety, equality of the sovereignty, non-acquisition of land by force and nonintervention in internal affairs; and an obligation to settle disputes by peaceful means."

This statement is incongruous when you realize that Egypt and Syria, nations that have launched numerous aggressive offenses against Israel, now say that they want to "settle disputes by peaceful means." Their seeming condemnation of Israel for its "acquisition of land by force" is ironic as well, considering that Egypt and Syria started every war from which Israel has ever gained territory.

Recent meetings of the Damascus Declaration countries have produced more of the same rhetoric. At one such meeting in 1996, the member nations praised Syria for their efforts to establish peace with Israel only under the condition that Israel withdraw fully from the Golan Heights. They also stated that Israel should join the Nuclear Proliferation Treaty and open its nuclear facilities up to inspection. Nuclear weapons might be the only deterrent that keeps Israel's Arab neighbors from attacking en masse. Finally, the member nations again called for the guarantee of political and national rights for the Palestinian people.

The bottom line of the Damascus Declaration is a written guarantee for the safety and rights of the Palestinian people, backed by the coalition formed between Syria and

Egypt. In other words, if the Israeli government was to make any decision that would harm the Palestinians or not allow them to have the rights that the Arab world believed they should have, then this declaration between Syria and Egypt would allow them to be in a position to guarantee these rights for the Palestinians, even if it required military action against Israel.

Daniel's Prophecy

It is quite interesting to note that twenty-five hundred years before the Damascus Declaration was ever signed, the Prophet Daniel spoke of an agreement of cooperation between Syria and Egypt. Daniel 11, one of the most prophetic chapters in all of God's Word, talks about five personalities that will come to power. The first one named is Ahasuerus, and Daniel prophesied his leadership, fifty-seven years before he actually came to power.

In Daniel 11:3-9, he talks about Alexander the Great who would be a mighty king; and when he died, his kingdom would be divided into four parts. One of those divisions would be led by Antiochus the Great. The prophecy of Antiochus the Great is found in verses 10 through 20. Daniel wrote about Antiochus taking power three hundred and thirty years before he actually did take control. In verses 21 through 35, Daniel reveals the pre-written history of Antiochus Epiphanes, who came to power three hundred and sixty years after Daniel wrote about him. In great detail, Daniel had prophesied that these four personalities would come to power, and—down to the minutest detail—these prophecies were all fulfilled.

From verses 36 through 45 in Daniel 11, the prophet talks about a fifth man who will come to power and his name is the "Antichrist." Verse 36 says,

"The king shall do according to his will;" the willful king. It describes how the Antichrist will come to power and he will honor the *"[g]od of forces"* (verse 38) most likely meaning that he will have control of a major military power.

It goes on to give detailed information about the Antichrist. In verse 40, Daniel begins to lay out what the Antichrist is going to do at the *"time of the end,"* in connection with the coalition of two nations coming together. The phrase, "time of the end," is speaking of the time when the Antichrist is on the world scene and Syria and Egypt have formed a formal coalition.

In Daniel 11:40-45, the prophet uses three pronouns: "he," "him," and "his." The word "he" is used seven times, the word "him" is used four times, and the word "his" is used three times for a total of fourteen times. Each time these pronouns are used, they are used in connection with the Antichrist.

At The Time Of The End

This passage also tells us at which time this prophecy will be fulfilled. In verse 40 it says, *"And at the time of the end."* This phrase is also used in Daniel 11:35, when he talks about the *"time of the end."* Then in chapter 12, verse 4, Daniel uses this same phrase; Daniel is to shut up the words and seal the book of the prophecy till the *"time of the end."* Now, at the "time of the end," we open up Daniel's prophecy and we see what he wrote twenty-five hundred years ago. What Daniel wrote was history, but he wrote it before it ever happened. That which the prophet foretold is coming onto the world's stage, even at this time. Daniel 11:40 says that, *"at the time of the end shall the king of the south push at him: and the king of the north shall come against him."* Here we have three personalities: "the king of the south," "the king of the north," and "him," the Antichrist.

Alexander the Great, a military and administrative genius, led the Greek-Macedonian Army in conquest of the Medo-Persian Empire in 334 B.C. This young military strategist was able to rule and conquer a vast territory, becoming the ruler of the known ancient world, only to be cut down by death at age thirty-two in 323 B.C.

True to Daniel's prophetic word, four Greek generals divided Alexander's kingdom into four parts, but none of them ever ruled with the same authority as Alexander. Of the four divisions of Alexander's kingdom, only two proved to be significant in the ancient world. One was headquartered in Egypt, under the rule of the Ptolemies, and the other was headquartered in Syria, ruled by the Seleucids.

Geographically, Egypt lies south of Israel; therefore, Daniel referred to the king who would be ruling Egypt at that time as "the king of the south." And since Syria was north of Israel, naturally the king of Syria at the time prophesied was known as "the king of the north." Thus, we can conclude that Daniel's prophecies of *"the king of the south"* and *"the king of the north"* in Daniel 11:40 are referring to modern-day Egypt and Syria.

Daniel foresaw the future at the time of the end, when Syria and Egypt would form a coalition and come together to attack "him." Remember that the pronouns "he," "his," and "him" in verses 40 through 45 are referring to Antichrist. The question then is, "How will Syria and Egypt attack the Antichrist at the time of the end?"

Antichrist To The Rescue

Let me remind you that the Antichrist will not appear on earth until after the Church has been raptured and the Revived Roman Empire is in place. The Antichrist comes out of the Revived Roman Empire (Daniel 7:8 and 24), and confirms a peace treaty between the Jewish people and their enemies (Daniel 9:27). Through the relationship developed between the false messiah, the Antichrist, and the Jewish people, this world-ruler will feel obligated to protect the Jewish people.

Antichrist will regard any attack upon Israel as an attack upon himself. As Syria and Egypt attack Israel, in a joint invasion from the north and the south, Antichrist will prepare to come to the aid of his Middle Eastern ally. The Antichrist will believe that he must leave his place of leadership over the "one-world church" headquartered in Rome and enter "the glorious land," the land of Israel, to defend the Jewish people.

Is the world stage set right now for all of this to unfold according to the prophetic scenario of the Bible? Absolutely. It is possible for Daniel's prophecy to be fulfilled today with the situation as it is in the Middle East. It is not only possible, but also very probable, that it could all come together very soon.

Syria has the fifth largest military power in the known world. Today, they have enhanced their military might with the assistance of Russian technology and technicians who have recently been in Syria. Russia has increased Syria's range for the Scuds they bought after the Gulf War, thirty-nine Scud-C missiles purchased from North Korea. There are reports that these Scud-C missiles have been placed in the Bekaa Valley, just north of the Israeli-Syrian border, aimed at the City of Jerusalem.

With Russia's help, the Syrians have been able to expand the range of these missiles all the way to the city of Eilat on the Red Sea, at the southern tip of Israel. In addition, Russia has given Syria the capability of using chemical warfare and producing the needed chemicals. They have upgraded their tank force with the latest technology. These tanks are now top-of-the-line fighting machines.

It has also been reported that Syria's elite commando units have been perched on Israel's northern border, on Mount Hermon, anticipating orders to come into Israel with an attack from the north. Looking at the negotiations going on, or should we say, negotiations that are *not* going on at this time between the Israelis and the Syrians, one can better understand why there is anticipation in Israel for an "invasion from the north."

The Golan Heights

President Basher Assad, who replaced his late father and Syria's longtime leader Hafaz Assad, would like to once again have control of the Golan Heights. In fact, he would like the entire Golan Heights reaching down to the shores of the Sea of Galilee. He has made a promise, as his father did, that if indeed he controlled the Golan Heights, which Syria did prior to 1967, he would give the Israelis peace. It's interesting to note, however, that from 1948 to 1967, the period when the Syrians did control the Golan Heights, there were three major wars that took place.

When Israel won its statehood in 1948, it captured and settled all the area leading right up to the Golan

Heights. In the time between the War of Independence in 1948 and the Six-Day War in 1967, Syria erected a vast network of defenses along the Golan Heights. These military positions were used to harass Israeli settlements that were in very vulnerable positions at the base of the Golan Heights. The Syrian Army would bombard these settlements with tank and artillery fire and effectively hold the Israelis hostage.

One of the Israeli settlements that was hit the hardest during that time was Kibbutz Ein Gev, situated on the shores of the Sea of Galilee. To this day you can still meet many people living on this Kibbutz who lost loved ones during those wanton acts of destruction. They can also tell you stories of children meeting for school in concrete bunkers and sleepless nights without electricity, waiting to see if the next shell would land on them.

Because of the constant threat to Israeli citizens and the security that the Golan Heights provided by acting as a buffer zone between Israel and Syria, Israel's Minister of Defense, General Moshe Dayan, decided that Israel needed to take the Golan Heights in 1967. Over a two-day period of intense fighting, Israel captured them and has retained control ever since. Most of the Israelis living in the north feel that the Golan Heights are crucial to their safety because they remember what Syria did when it had control of the area.

The "King Of The South"

But Syria is only half of the equation in the Damascus Declaration. Egypt, the "king of the south," is a major player in the alignment of the nations against Israel in the last days. Though Egypt is not quite the military power that Syria is, they still are a force to be reckoned with. What Egypt brings to the table is a mass of humanity. They have the largest population of any of the Arab countries, and they are growing by leaps and bounds.

The present population figures indicate that Egypt is at sixty-five million people and grows by an additional one million every six months. This sizable population allows Egypt to have a very large call-up military. Today, Egypt has the potential military manpower to provide seventeen million males between the ages of 15 and 49 for combat duty. This large amount of Egyptian personnel available to go to war is three times the size of the total Jewish population in Israel.

The "king of the south," Egypt, has been involved in military maneuvers in the Sinai in the last year-and-a-half, raising the question, "Why?" Maybe the answer lies in the fact that Egypt is ready to go to war with their so-called peace partner. The Camp David Accords never have been normalized between the two countries. The visits by government officials from Russia, promising new military technology and the technicians to assist in preparing to fight a regional war, send a signal that something may be up.

Egypt's advanced plans for war against Israel were outlined in an extensive article recently in one of Israel's leading newspapers. According to the article, "Egypt's war plans have been discussed and boasted about openly by top members of the country's security establishment."

It is public knowledge that during Egypt's largest-ever military exercise in the fall of 1996, their Defense Minister Muhammad Dantawi told reporters straight out that the training was in preparation for an upcoming war with Israel.

There are reports detailing Egypt's increased levels

of arms—both in quality and quantity—in air, rocket, naval, and ground power. According to some sources, the Egyptian military has become increasingly advanced, thanks in part to more sophisticated U.S. tanks which the Americans not only provided, but trained the Egyptians to build independently. These tanks surpass those of Israel on a number of counts.

You may wonder why a newspaper, and not the political establishment, is disseminating this information. Quite simply, the Israeli people don't even want to consider the idea of going to war with Egypt. Public sentiment is 'Why risk disturbing one of the only peace treaties with a neighboring Arab state?' And with the public so unwilling to confront the matter, politicians are afraid to even raise the issue.

This hesitation to upset people's perceptions reminds me of the facts surrounding the Yom Kippur War in 1993 between Egypt and Israel. No one wanted to think that a war between these two countries would really happen, but it did. The Yom Kippur War was devastating to Israel. Before the Israeli Defense Forces could get armed and ready to fight, Israel suffered great human losses.

The "king of the north" and "the king of the south"—Syria and Egypt—are both armed and ready to go to war with their Jewish neighbor, Israel. The Damascus Declaration has formed the coalition that the Prophet Daniel speaks about and it has given them a written document that the world will accept as the basis for attacking Israel.

The Revived Roman Empire is about to take form through the infrastructure of the European Union. All the actors are in place for the next scene to begin.

Chapter 10
Ezekiel's Coalition

A unique experience in my life has been the privilege to co-host the Day of Discovery television program with Mart DeHaan. We recently had the opportunity to go into Turkey to do a series of videos that covered the messages to the seven churches of Revelation, recorded in chapters 2 and 3; the seven churches of Asia Minor.

While we were there doing the television shoot, we ran across an ancient Turkish map. I am very interested in studying maps, since I know that geography is a key ingredient in understanding prophecy. As I was studying this map, I noticed that Meshech, Tubal, Gomer, and Togarmah were part of what we know as modern-day Turkey. Listed on this ancient map of Asia Minor were these four different locations.

Remember that Meshech, Tubal, Gomer, and Togarmah go back to Genesis 10, and were grandsons of Noah, the sons of Japheth. It is in the last days that they will appear in prophecy. Our task will be to determine where these particular Biblical locations are in the modern-day world. You must understand that when God was giving these prophecies to Ezekiel, He was naming peoples and locations that existed in Ezekiel's time.

Daniel's Prophecy

This brings us to a coalition of nations that will come against Israel in the end times. This alliance of nations the Prophet Ezekiel describes is first mentioned in Daniel 11, right after Daniel speaks of the coalition between the *"king of the north"* (Syria) and the *"king of the south"* (Egypt) (Daniel 11:40). Daniel concludes his prophecy about Syria and Egypt in chapter 11, verse 43, *"But he shall have power"*—speaking of "he", the Antichrist—*"over the treasures of gold and of silver, and over all the precious things of Egypt."*

The Antichrist comes into the glorious Holy Land. He goes into the north, and basically destroys Syria. He moves through Jordan, but does not touch Jordan. He goes into the south, and destroys Egypt. Antichrist then turns around and starts back to Jerusalem (Daniel 11:40-43). The Antichrist is not finished, as we see in verse 43: *"And the Libyans and the Ethiopians shall be at his steps."*

As Antichrist turns around to go back to Jerusalem to set up his kingdom on the Temple Mount, at his steps will be the Libyans and the Ethiopians. Then verse 44 says, *"But tidings out of the east and out of the north."* Remember, in the Bible, God uses Jerusalem as the center point of all direction. The Libyans are located west of Jerusalem, and the Ethiopians are in the south.

The other two directions, north and east, are now mentioned in verse 44 and thus nations from the four different directions surrounding Israel are going to form a coalition to come against this modern-day Jewish state in the last days. Ezekiel's prophecy in chapter 38 is part of a series of messages or prophecies that God gave to Ezekiel after the destruction of the City of Jerusalem during the Babylonian captivity.

Ezekiel's Prophecy

The message of "retribution" in the first thirty-two chapters of Ezekiel, now becomes a message of "restoration" in the last sixteen chapters of the book. In chapters 33 through 39, Ezekiel talks about a restoration of the "kingdom people," the Jewish people. God is also going to restore to them their land. In chapter 34, eighteen times He says, "I will": *"I will"* reach into the countries of the world, and *"I will"* bring them out, and *"I will"* give them the land of their forefathers.

In chapter 35, Ezekiel talks about a people that will rise up in the last days to try to take the land away from the Jewish people. In chapter 36, thirty-five different times He mentions the land and His commitment to keep His promise to give the Jewish people the land. In chapter 37, Ezekiel conveys the message or prophecy of the valley of the dry bones, where He speaks of reaching into the world and bringing the Jewish people back into the land from the four corners of the earth.

Then, with the Jewish people returned to a land that God is in the process of restoring, in chapter 38 there is a coalition of nations which will come together with an army to attack Israel from all four sides: north, south, east, and west. Ezekiel 38:1-2 says, *"And the word of the Lord came unto me, saying, Son of man, set thy face against Gog, the land of Magog."*

Gog is the leader of the nations mentioned in verse 2; he's referred to as the ruler or prince of the nations. And Magog is the land from where Gog comes to power. There is a nation, not mentioned in some Bible translations as a nation, but as another title describing Gog. That nation is defined by the Hebrew word "Rosh," which has been interpreted "chief" by some translators. The true meaning of the word "Rosh" is derived from a close study of history, as well as other uses of the word in the Bible.

Modern-Day Locations

To determine the modern-day locations of the

nations listed in Ezekiel 38 we must go back in history. I will not do an exhaustive study of that history, but instead direct you to a book written by Mark Hitchcock, titled *After the Empire*, for extensive historical background on these nations. What I offer now are the end conclusions of his studies. These conclusions will help us to identify the ten nations mentioned by the Prophet Ezekiel in his prophecy, in their modern-day status.

Magog. Magog is today the area that was once the homeland of the Scythians, mentioned by the Apostle Paul in Colossians 3:11. Throughout their history, the Scythians are described as a warlike, viciously cruel, barbaric people who inhabited central Asia and the southern part of Russia. Today, central Asia is inhabited by the former Soviet republics of Kazakhstan, Kirghizia, Uzbekistan, Turkmenistan, Tajikistan, and the Ukraine.

Rosh. "Rosh," the Hebrew word translated "chief" in the King James Version of the Bible (Ezekiel 38:2) and in other translations, should designate Rosh as one of the nations that will align itself against Israel.

While there are arguments for Rosh to be translated "chief," the great weight of evidence favors taking Rosh as a proper name of a geographical location. The *Septuagint*, the Greek translation of the Old Testament, translates the Hebrew "rosh" as the proper name Rosh. This is significant since the *Septuagint* was translated only three centuries after the Book of Ezekiel was written.

From history we have background information of the ancient Sarmatians, who were known as "Ros" or "Rus" and are the people Ezekiel called Rosh in his prophecy. Ancient history gives evidence that seems to make it very clear that Rosh is Russia. The ancient people of Rosh inhabited the former southern republics of the U.S.S.R. and Russia. The Scythians of Magog and the Sarmatians of Rosh indicate that Ezekiel's coalition includes modern-day Russia.

Meshech. A study of the history of Meshech, first mentioned in Genesis 10 as the grandson of Noah, reveals that in Persian times, which was approximately thirty to fifty years after Ezekiel wrote, Meshech was located near the southeast part of the Black Sea. This area southeast of the Black Sea is clearly in the modern nation of Turkey. Ezekiel also includes Meshech's brother Tubal in the list of nations.

Tubal. Tubal, another grandson of Noah (Genesis 10:2), and Meshech were closely related to one another in ancient history. As sons of Japheth, these two had very similar historical backgrounds. In addition, at every point in the history of Meshech and Tubal, these two nations occupied territory in what we know today as the modern nation of Turkey, southeast of the Black Sea. To ascribe any other location to them is inconsistent with the clear facts of ancient history.

Gomer. In the sixth verse of chapter 38, Ezekiel mentions two other nations that have a close relationship, Gomer and Togarmah. Their relationship dates back to right after the Flood (Genesis 10:2-3) when Gomer was born the first son of Japheth and Togarmah was born as the third son of Gomer. It's also interesting to note that Gomer had three brothers named Magog, Meshech, and Tubal.

Historians believe that Gomer eventually settled in the area of Cappadocia, which today is in central and north-central Turkey. The historical works of Josephus say that the people the Greeks called the Galatians, in New Testament times, were the Gomerites, living in the central area of modern

Turkey. This can be traced down through history. But what about Gomer's son, Togarmah?

Togarmah. The only evidence in the Bible of the location of Togarmah is Ezekiel's statement in chapter 38, verse 6: from the remote parts *"of the north."* Turkey is to the north of Israel and could fit the description of the location for Togarmah. Most Bible scholars and scholars of ancient history relate Togarmah to Tegarma, the ancient Hittite city, an important city in eastern Cappadocia, modern-day Turkey. While scholars differ slightly on the exact location, they always place Togarmah within the boundaries of the modern nation of Turkey.

Persia. Another ally of Gog during the invasion of Israel is Persia, the easiest of the nations in Ezekiel 38 to locate. Written all over the pages of history is the name "Persia," a name changed to Iran in foreign usage in March 1935. On this point there is universal agreement. Iran will join forces with Turkey and Russia to attack Israel in the last days.

Cush-Ethiopia. The King James translation of the Bible identifies the next partner in the "Gog coalition" as Ethiopia. In the Hebrew language and other Biblical translations, the name "Cush" is used to describe the nation. Hebrew scholars locate Cush in the area south of Egypt, and that location is substantiated in the Old Testament. The proper name "Cush" is used thirty times in the Old Testament, which locates Cush south of Egypt. This would identify the ancient nation of Cush as the modern nations of Sudan and Ethiopia.

Put-Libya. The final ally in the coalition is referred to as Libya by the King James Version of the Bible, giving us a shortcut in determining the actual location of the Hebrew "Put." Josephus says that Put was the founder of Libya, located in Africa, which is where other Biblical scholars place Put. The *Septuagint* also renders the word Put as "Libues," an ancient name for Libya. We can be quite certain that the King James Bible is right in calling Put the modern nation of Libya.

These nations will become the "Ezekiel coalition" which will come against Israel in the last days: Russia and the republics of the former Soviet Union in the north; Ethiopia and Sudan in the south; Libya in the west; and Iran in the east. Turkey, made up of Meshech, Tubal, Gomer, and Togarmah, coming also from the north, will join the "Ezekiel coalition" for the slaughter of the Jews in Israel.

Turkey's Coalition

Someone might question how Turkey will be a part of this coalition, in light of the deepening military ties between Israel and Turkey. Recent reports indicate that Turkey, Israel, and the United States held military exercises in the Mediterranean. These were search-and-rescue naval operations, non-combative military exercises, but there was a show of a relationship between these three countries.

At a recent Islamic conference held in Iran, the Turkish government, led by President Suleyman Demirel, left the conference—and the coalition of Islamic nations—when they started going after Israel. Those at the Islamic conference denounced Turkey, as a partner militarily with the nation of Israel.

Turkey is ninety-nine percent Islamic, though it be a secular Islamic faith that guides Turkey. However, there is an Islamic fundamentalist movement in Turkey that is becoming stronger every day. They are part of a larger movement that desires to establish an Islamic fundamentalist national leadership in the nations of this Middle Eastern region.

The only thing that is keeping Turkey from becoming a full-blown Islamic Republic is the Turkish military. The military believes that they are the guardians or the custodians of the secular Islamic faith in Turkey. Turkey's secular government, however, could quickly be swept aside, placing the Turkish nation in a position to become part of this Ezekiel 38 coalition.

Iran

About two years ago, Libya and Iran formed a partnership by contributing funding to the development of a long-range Scud missile. They approached North Korea to help them develop this missile. The North Koreans came up with a long-range Scud missile capable of carrying some type of a warhead, be it nuclear, biological, or chemical. Both Libya and Iran purchased these long-range Scud missiles and thus formed a partnership, just a step away from a coalition.

It is widely known, especially through Israeli intelligence, that Russian technicians and technology has been transferred to Iran. In fact, this Russian technology has been used to develop a long-range missile that would give Iran the capability of launching a Scud missile from Tehran, Iran, with a range that would take it to an exact target in Jerusalem. This missile also has a range capable of reaching into Western Europe, and they are working on a Scud that would have the capability to reach all the way to the United States.

This technology has not only produced and developed a long-range Scud that could carry a nuclear warhead, but it is helping to develop the nuclear warhead. The Israeli intelligence report said that there could be a nuclear warhead, or chemical and biological warheads, within six months. These warheads could be mounted on the long-range Scud missiles that would then carry these weapons into the state of Israel.

Benjamin Netanyahu, when prime minister of Israel, as well as the then Defense Minister Yitzak Mordecai, made public announcements that Iran was the number one threat to the Israelis in the Middle East. While on a Middle East visit, U.S. Secretary of Defense William Cohen confirmed this analysis of Iran.

This determination was made on the basis that Iran is not interested in the peace process; in fact, they want to do everything possible to discourage the peace process. It has been their money that has funded most of the terrorist activities that have taken place in the Middle East. It is Iran's money and munitions coming into Damascus, Syria, that are transported to the Islamic terrorist organization Hizbollah which is located at the northern border of Israel in that buffer zone in southern Lebanon.

The goal and desire of Hizbollah is to do everything they possibly can to destroy the nation of Israel and to disperse the Jews out of the Middle East. Hizbollah, in partnership with Iran and Syria, has been able to move very close to fulfilling their goals. Their coalition is intact and all of these activities are taking place in light of what the Scriptures had to say some twenty-five hundred years ago.

Dwelling In Peace

As we look at Ezekiel 38, we are able to discern at least a time period when these things will take place. Ezekiel 38:8 describes the time when the coalition of nations will come together to attack Israel. Verse 8 says, *"After many days thou shalt be visited: in the latter years thou shalt come into the land that is brought back from the sword, and is gathered out of many people, against the mountains of Israel, which have been*

*always waste: but it is brought forth out of the nations,
and they shall dwell safely all of them."*

When God reaches into the nations of the world,
when that aliya of the Jewish people takes place and
they are gathered out of the nations of the world, they
come back into the land, and will become a nation and
dwell safely in the land. This gives us an indicator as to
the time for the fulfillment of the prophecy of Ezekiel.
It will be during that peaceful period of time when the
Antichrist comes to power in the seven-year
Tribulation. At the very first of the seven years, he
establishes a peace between Israel and her enemies.
Antichrist will make the Jewish people feel that they are
living safely in the land of Israel.

Ezekiel 38:11 says, *"Thou shall say, I will go up to
the land of unwalled villages; I will go to them that are
at rest, that dwell safely, all of them dwelling without
walls, and having neither bars nor gates."* Verse 11 is
referring to a military term when it uses the phrase,
"unwalled villages." The time of the attack will be so
marked when the enemies of Israel come to a Jewish
nation living with unwalled cities.

Today, there are no walls around the state of Israel,
but in the time of Ezekiel a walled city was a defensive
military apparatus used to defend a particular nation
from its enemies. When Israel lays down their military
defense system—when they are at rest, living in an area
of unwalled villages—that will be the time of attack by
the coalition.

Israel's Military Strategy

During the Gulf Crisis, the United States
government pressured the Israeli government not to
retaliate against Iraq while under attack. This was
contrary to the military strategy of the Jewish people

for four thousand years. During those four thousand years Israel's military strategy has basically been two-pronged. First of all, when under attack, they would take the enemy and return to the homeland of the enemy and there they would fight. The Jewish people don't want to fight in their own land so they go into the land of their enemy and fight there.

The second prong of the strategy was that they would go immediately for the jugular, to take out their attacking enemy. They don't want to play around or prolong the fighting; therefore, the Israeli military uses the force needed to end the fighting. Someone asked me during the Gulf Crisis, "How long would the war have lasted had Israel been involved?" My response: "About fifteen minutes." They would have sent one of their jets to land in Baghdad. They would have dispersed a commando unit to go into the palace of Saddam Hussein. And finally, they would have cut off his head and thrown it in the sand of the desert.

The Israeli government was ready: the F16s were on the ramp, the cockpits were manned, the canopies on the jets were down, the engines were running—but the pilots' feet were on the brakes. Had Iraq advanced beyond the red line, a military term in Israel for going too far, those jets would have taken off and there would have been retaliation.

Israel's Protection

During the Gulf Crisis, in light of the fact that they did not retaliate, the question was asked, "Why not?" What gave Israel the confidence to believe that they would be protected? The United States government came to Israel and pressured them not to fight back. During that time, as a journalist, I approached two different U.S. Secretaries of State, James Baker and

Lawrence Eagleberger, on why they were putting this pressure on Israel. Their answer was that they would put up Patriot missile sites all over Israel to protect the Israelis from those incoming Scuds that Saddam Hussein was firing.

Out of thirty-nine Scud attacks on Israel, only one Scud was brought down by a Patriot missile and the Israelis are not fully convinced that even that one Scud was destroyed. While visiting at the Israeli President's house two years ago, I spoke with Moshe Arens, who was the Defense Minister during the Gulf Crisis, and I asked him if indeed the Patriot missiles had been successful in defending the land of Israel.

Arens said that there had been a report that one Patriot brought down one Scud, but he was not sure if that was true. He exclaimed that the Patriot missiles had been absolutely useless as a defense mechanism for the Israeli people. But the Israeli people were psyched into believing that they were being protected, so they laid down their defenses, their military might. The Israelis were of a mindset that they were living in the "unwalled villages" talked about in Ezekiel 38. They were dwelling safely, resting upon someone else to take care of meeting their security needs.

Why did this happen? I believe that God allowed it to happen to prepare the Jewish people for someone who says he can protect them. The "protector" will be able to provide the security for the Jewish people to live in "unwalled cities." Ezekiel 38:12 says that when this happens, the enemy will come to take a "spoil": *"To take a spoil, and to take a prey; to turn thine hand upon the desolate places that are now inhabited, and upon the people that are gathered out of the nations, which have gotten cattle and goods, that dwell in the midst of the land."*

Hooks In Their Jaws

The prophecy speaks of a time when the land of Israel has been returned to the Jews, and they have established a nation. The verse continues to say that when they have cultivated the land, and are raising the cattle, that's when the enemies come. Beef cattle are now grazing throughout the land, in places like Mount Carmel and in the Golan Heights. The coalition of nations comes when the Jews are in the land developing a prospering nation.

This coalition of nations will come to take a spoil from Israel because they seem to be so prosperous. Ezekiel says that the Lord will *"put hooks"* in their jaws, and bring them forth (Ezekiel 38:4). The "hooks" may well be the need for the riches of the land of Israel. Going through the list of nations, in particular Russia, they have many needs, thus reasons to want to take a spoil from Israel. Russia needs a warm water port for their Navy and shipping industry. They need access to foodstuffs, both fruits and vegetables. Israel could supply both of these needs.

As I write this chapter there is an intense search for oil going on in Israel. There was an important discovery of natural gas made off the coast of Ashkelon in the Mediterranean. First reports are that it could supply all of Israel's needs for the next fifteen years. There are also operations at the southern end of the Dead Sea looking for crude oil. Some geologists believe that region could produce a major oil find.

The prospects for oil in Israel, natural resources from the Dead Sea, a more productive agricultural operation, and the location of the nation—a "land bridge" between three continents—makes Israel "ripe for the picking." God will use the needs of the attacking nations and the resources of Israel as the "hook" to bring these nations into Israel.

Some have questioned whether the breakup of the former Soviet Union has set back the time of fulfillment of Ezekiel 38. Quite the contrary. With the failure of communism in the Soviet Union the prospects for fulfilled prophecy have gotten better. Remember that the republics in the region around Russia are now quickly becoming "Islamic Republics." The Islamic influence in the area of all the nations mentioned by Ezekiel only enhances the possibility of fulfillment, very soon.

Chapter 11
The Bully of Baghdad

It was 2 a.m. in the morning when I was jarred from a sound sleep by a siren warning of an incoming Iraqi Scud. Judy and I hurriedly moved toward the sealed room that we had prepared for refuge in the event of a military attack. After taking time to quickly answer a telephone call, we ran into the sealed room, which we hoped would protect us from the incoming Scud. I sealed the door behind me with sheets of tape, covering any potential openings through which gases or chemicals in the warhead of the incoming Scud might enter the room.

As we sat in the sealed room putting on our gas masks, I was reminded of what Saddam Hussein had said earlier in the year, when he had promised to gas half of Israel. Would he now make good on his promise?

The procedure for putting on the gas mask was to take your canister out, attach it to your gas mask, and then put the gas mask on, making certain it was sealed on all sides so nothing could get under the mask to contaminate your breathing. Once prepared, with our gas masks on, we just sat there praying for God's watch care over us. It was a very eerie feeling for Judy and me. We sat there for five hours, never removing the gas masks, anticipating what might happen. All we could think about was what is wrong with this man—the bully of Baghdad, Saddam Hussein—who wanted to gas innocent people, and in particular the Jewish people of Israel?

Now, under attack, we were better able to understand Saddam's thinking, a man who believes he is the reincarnation of Nebuchadnezzar. Indeed, he was carrying on the heritage of a people who were truly the only ones able to defeat Israel and take them out of their land and remove them from the selected spot that God had given them. Indeed, prophecy students realize that modern-day Iraq is Biblical Babylon.

Biblical Babylon

The name Babylon is used 266 times in the Bible, referring to that location on the Euphrates River, about sixty miles up from where the Tigris and Euphrates Rivers join together before they flow into the Persian Gulf. It was Babel, the same location where Nimrod, the mighty hunter before the Lord (Genesis 10:8-10), would go to build a great city and then a tower as a monument to his greatness.

It was in Babel, which would later become Babylon, where God divided the nations by giving them separate languages. Nimrod was a forerunner of Nebuchadnezzar who would also try to make Babylon the greatest city in all of the earth. Babylon was known as one of the wonders of the earth with its palaces, temples, and hanging gardens. Even until today, no one has been able to explain how those hanging gardens were constructed.

Living in Jerusalem in January 1991, we faced thirty-nine Scud attacks that originated in Iraq, Biblical Babylon. I would be reminded often during the Gulf Crisis that God had pronounced judgment upon these people. In fact, every time we took a taxi ride in Jerusalem we thought we were traveling with a prophecy teacher, as the taxi driver would turn around and start talking to us about what he considered the fulfillment of Jeremiah 50 and 51.

When asked about that, he would say that there is a

judgment pronounced by God on the Babylonians, modern-day Iraq, and it looks like the Gulf Crisis is going to be the fulfillment of that prophecy. However, while it was not the fulfillment of that prophecy, the prophecy will be fulfilled, yet in the future. For God has indeed pronounced judgment on Babylon, modern-day Iraq, in Jeremiah 50 and 51.

Babylon's Judgment

Jeremiah 50:13, says, *"Because of the wrath of the Lord [Babylon] shall not be inhabited, but it shall be wholly desolate: every one that goeth by Babylon shall be astonished, and hiss at all her plagues."* Verse 39 says, *"Therefore the wild beasts of the desert with the wild beasts of the islands shall dwell there, and the owls shall dwell therein: and it shall be no more inhabited for ever."* Those words, "for ever," are the Hebrew word "olam," which is the same word used to describe the eternality of God, meaning forever.

The land will be inhabited no more forever, neither shall anyone live in Babylon from generation to generation. Jeremiah 51:29 continues to pronounce God's judgment on Babylon: *"And the land shall tremble and sorrow: for every purpose of the Lord shall be performed against Babylon, to make the land of Babylon a desolation without an inhabitant."* Verse 37 says, *"And Babylon shall become heaps, a dwellingplace for dragons, an astonishment, and an hissing, without an inhabitant."*

Verse 43 says, *"Her cities are a desolation, a dry land, and a wilderness, a land wherein no man dwelleth, neither doth any son of man pass thereby."* Verse 62 says, *"Then shall thou say, O Lord, thou hast spoken against this place, to cut it off, that none shall remain in it, neither man nor beast, but that it shall be desolate for ever.* "

So, throughout chapters 50 and 51, the Prophet Jeremiah tells us that there is a coming judgment that has been pronounced upon Babylon. The reason for this coming judgment is the vengeance of God because of His temple. Specifically Jeremiah 50:28 states: *"The voice of them that flee and escape out of the land of Babylon, to declare in Zion the vengeance of the Lord our God, the vengeance of his temple."* Then again in 51:11, *"Make bright the arrows; gather the shields: the Lord hath raised up the spirit of the kings of the Medes: for his device is against Babylon, to destroy it; because it is the vengeance of the Lord, the vengeance of his temple."*

It is interesting to note why the Lord is pronouncing His vengeance on Babylon; it is because of His temple. Jeremiah 50:40 says, *"As God overthrew Sodom and Gomorrah and the neighbour cities thereof, saith the Lord; so shall no man abide there, neither shall any son of man dwell therein."* As He destroyed Sodom and Gomorrah, God has promised through the Prophet Jeremiah to destroy Babylon. And He says, it is *"the vengeance of the Lord [for]...his temple"* (Jeremiah 50:28).

Fall Of The Babylonian Empire

To understand the severity of this judgment we must go back to Daniel 5, to the story of the downfall of the Babylonian Empire. Belshazzar, the grandson of Nebuchadnezzar, the one who went to Jerusalem and destroyed the temple in 586 B.C., now leads the Babylonians. Belshazzar made a great feast for a thousand of his lords, and they drank wine before the thousands. They were having a drunken party in the palace in Babylon.

Belshazzar, while he tasted the wine, commanded

them to bring the gold and silver vessels, which his grandfather Nebuchadnezzar had taken out of the temple in Jerusalem. These were the vessels that were consecrated for use in the temple. Belshazzar, leader of the Babylonians, was desecrating them. They were using these sacred vessels for a drunken party that was taking place at the palace in Babylon. This happened just prior to the destruction of the Babylonian Empire.

Daniel 5 records the fall of the Babylonian Empire. Verses 30 and 31 say, *"In that night was Belshazzar the king of the Chaldeans slain. And Darius the Median took the kingdom,"* becoming head of the Medo-Persian Empire. Babylon was an impregnable city that was surrounded by two walls, each over 300 feet high and 87 feet wide; and a moat lay between them. In fact, the walls of Babylon were so wide the Babylonians could race two chariots on the top of them.

They had enough food in the city to last them for twenty years. They had all the water they needed because the Euphrates River flowed underneath the northern wall and exited out the southern wall. The Babylonians were set. They had an impregnable city that could not be captured. No army could safely come over two walls over 300 feet high, with a moat in between, and enter the city ready to fight.

What took place was that the Medes and the Persians went north on the Euphrates River and built a temporary dam to dry up the water. Then they went south and built another temporary dam, drying up the water underneath the walls. This action formed a tunnel beneath the walls, making it very convenient for the Medes and the Persians to enter the banquet hall and there kill Belshazzar, that night. But that was only the fall of the Babylonian Empire, not the fall of the city itself. In fact, the city of Babylon is alive and well today.

Babylon, Alive Today

The Apostle Peter wrote in his first book a comment about *"the church that is at Babylon"* (I Peter 5:13). Peter was in Babylon when he was writing to the people that were scattered abroad. While Peter was on his journey to preach the gospel to the uttermost parts of the earth, he visited the church in Babylon. At that time, Babylon was the second–most populated Jewish city in the world because of the Jews who had not returned to Israel after the Babylonian captivity.

There has never been a time when Babylon has not been inhabited. Today, within the boundaries of the city limits of Babylon itself, there are three small Arab villages. In addition to that, there is much construction that is going on there. This construction has been going on for quite a while now. I have a clipping from the *U.S.A. Today* newspaper, dated Friday, September 8, 1989. One of the little articles under "Elsewhere in the world" states that "Iraqi President Saddam Hussein is offering 1.5 million dollars to any citizen who can figure out how King Nebuchadnezzar watered the hanging gardens of Babylon."

Experts debate whether the gardens, said to be built in the sixth century B.C., even existed. Iraq believes they did. The Iraqi government is offering the prize for information to help in its project to rebuild the Mesopotamian city where Nebuchadnezzar ruled. Saddam Hussein, at least since 1989, has been endeavoring to reconstruct the city of Babylon.

On June 28, 1990, Judy and I were watching the ABC television program "Primetime America." Diane Sawyer, who is the host for this TV newsmagazine, was doing a one-hour special from Baghdad, where she was interviewing Saddam Hussein from his palace. During that program, they cut away for what is called a "sound bite" to the palace that Saddam Hussein was refurbishing, located in the city of Babylon.

Diane walked along the walls and pointed out a brick in the wall. "You see this brick, this was one of the bricks that Nebuchadnezzar had made for the original wall. His signature is on this brick," Sawyer said. Then she walked a little bit further and pointed out another brick that had Saddam Hussein's name printed on it. "These are the bricks that are being used to refurbish the city of Babylon today," she reported.

Later that year, on July 25, a CBS Morning News reporter was standing in Babylon, talking about the rebuilding of the city of Babylon. He said that the city was being rebuilt to establish Saddam Hussein as the rightful heir to Nebuchadnezzar. The city of Babylon is still in existence today. Those that live in the area are refurbishing the city.

President Bush's Connection

This story also has an interesting connection to President George Bush, who was president of the United States at the time of the Gulf Crisis. The night that he gave the command for the American forces to proceed with their attack on Iraq during the Gulf War, the president read a book given to him by world-renowned evangelist Dr. Billy Graham, who had come that evening to spend the night at the White House. George Bush read the book, *Armageddon, Oil and the Middle East Crisis*, written by Dr. John F. Walvoord.

After reading this book, he wanted copies of Dr. Walvoord's book distributed to his staff. Then the president gave an order to the Secretary of Defense, Dick Cheney, who passed the command along to the Chairman of the Joint Chiefs of Staff, Colin Powell.

Colin Powell then passed the command to Norman Schwarzkopf, the commander of the forces in the Gulf Crisis: none of the sacred Biblical sites were to be destroyed during the air raids in Iraq. In particular, they were not to bomb the construction work in the city of Babylon.

Babylon's Future

As we think about the alignment of the nations, one of the nations we should be watching is Iraq. The city of Babylon will become a great power center. The Bible tells us that the next time Babylon is built up, it will be the economic power center of the world at the time of the end. Revelation 18 talks about a false economy that will be headquartered in a city called Babylon.

The word "Babylon" is used three times in Revelation 18. Verse 2 says, *"Mightily with a strong voice, saying, Babylon the great is fallen."* Then in verse 10, *"Standing afar off for the fear of her torment, saying, Alas, alas, that great city Babylon, that mighty city"* will be destroyed. Verse 21 says, *"And a mighty angel took up a stone like a great millstone, and cast it into the sea, saying, Thus with violence shall that great city Babylon be thrown down, and shall be found no more at all."*

The word "city" is used seven times in Revelation 18, referring to an actual city that will be the economic center of the world and also the seat of the Antichrist, who will be headquartered in this city. The Antichrist will come into power over a one-world religion, referred to in Revelation 17. Though the word "Babylon" is used in chapter 17, it is referring to the false religiosity that began at Babylon over four thousand years ago. It is not the same as the "city" of chapter 18.

Power is transferred from the one-world church, headquartered in the city of Rome, to the Revived Roman Empire, referred to in Revelation 17:16. The "ten horns," which Daniel 7 defines as the Revived Roman Empire, shall hate the "whore," the false church. The Revived Roman Empire *"shall make her"*—the false church—*"desolate and naked, and shall eat her flesh, and burn her with fire"* (Revelation 17:16). In other words, the Revived Roman Empire will destroy the one-world church whose center of operations is in the city of Rome.

Revelation 17:17 says, *"For God hath put in their hearts to fulfil his will, and to agree, and give their kingdom unto the beast, until the words of God shall be fulfilled."* God is going to allow evil men to accomplish His will. The power is now given to Satan and he moves from the city of seven hills, Rome, Italy, into the city of Babylon to establish a one-world economy.

Revelation 17 refers to an ecclesiastical Babylon, or false religiosity, worldwide. Then there is an economic Babylon in chapter 18, which is a false worldwide economy. Babylon will become headquarters not only for the worldwide economy, but it will be the headquarters for the Antichrist to launch his intense attacks against Israel.

Revelation 12 and 13 talk about the future event defined as the battle between the good angels and the evil angels, when Satan is thrown out of Heaven. At that time Satan empowers the Antichrist. They join forces and intensify their attacks against the Jewish people. With the Antichrist headquartered in Babylon, it now becomes the center of the military operations for attacks against Israel.

Babylon is in position to become a great economic power. It is located on the Euphrates River in modern-day Iraq. During the Gulf Crisis, Saddam Hussein crossed the border and took control of Kuwait. His goal was to go in and take control of Saudi Arabia. That was the main reason the nations came together and formed a coalition, to protect Saudi Arabia and their massive oil fields that would have been under the control of this bully of Baghdad had he been successful.

If Saddam had been able to go into Saudi Arabia and had taken control of those oil fields, he would have controlled sixty-three percent of the oil deposits of this world. Many economists have said that anyone who controls sixty-three percent of the oil deposits of this world could control the economies of the world. That which the Bible predicted, the economies of this world being controlled from Babylon, is not only possible, but it is going to happen.

Upon reflection one must realize that the Gulf Crisis was only a "dry-run" for the prophetic scenario of God's Word being fulfilled. Saddam Hussein may well pass from the world scene, but there will be someone, someone even worse than the bully of Baghdad, who will lead Iraq (Biblical Babylon) to the conclusion of God's pre-written history. Iraq will align itself against Israel in the last days.

TREND 3
Anticipation

Chapter 12
Anticipation for Peace

For the last nine years, I have lived in the land of Israel as a journalist. I am aware of the continuing peace process between Israel and its enemies. To the world, both parties have been trying to come to a negotiating table to develop a comprehensive peace for the Arabs and the Jews, so they can coexist in the Middle East. The Bible indicates that there will not be a true peace until the time of the end.

Camp David Accords

Before coming to Israel to live, I was very interested in the Camp David Accords and the process that brought about this peace agreement between Egypt and Israel in 1979. As a student of prophecy, I had studied about a time when the Antichrist would sign a peace agreement with Israel. I understood that such an agreement would start the clock for the seven-year period of time known as the Tribulation.

After the Camp David Accords were signed and it was announced to the world that there was now peace between Israel and Egypt, I received a phone call from a friend asking me if this was this the peace agreement talked about in Daniel 9:27. I told him that I did not believe the Camp David Accords was the agreement prophesied by Daniel.

The Oslo Accords

On September 13, 1993, Judy and I sat in the Government Press Office in Jerusalem, watching on a big screen television the signing of the Oslo Accords between Israel's Prime Minister Yitzhak Rabin and the Chairman of the Palestinian people, Yasser Arafat. As I witnessed this happening, I realized another peace agreement was on the table. When I returned to my apartment in Jerusalem, another friend called to ask if this was the peace agreement that Daniel had talked about. Again, I told this friend that I did not believe the Oslo Accords was the peace treaty that would start the seventieth week of Daniel.

Israeli-Jordanian Peace Treaty

As a journalist, I had the unique experience of covering the signing of the peace agreement between Israel and Jordan. I traveled to Eilat, the southernmost city in Israel, located on the Red Sea, where the signing ceremony took place. On October 26, 1994, the Israel-Jordan Peace Treaty was signed by Prime Minister Yitzhak Rabin of Israel and King Hussein of Jordan; United States President Bill Clinton was also in attendance to witness this historic event.

I drove right back to Jerusalem after the ceremony, and yet another friend called me to ask if this was the peace agreement to be signed between the Antichrist and the Jewish people. Once again, I said that I did not believe it was that particular peace agreement. Soon after that, I started to reflect on what God's Word actually says. I decided to study again Daniel 9:27, which tells us of an anticipated peace that will come about through a world ruler called the Antichrist. This will be a false peace, established for a short time.

The True Peace

The word "peace" is on the lips of every politician

throughout the world who wants to play a role in the peace process in the Middle East. There is this anticipation for peace in our world today. The Bible talks about the Prince of Peace who will return and establish a "true peace" in the world. This anticipation for peace in our thoughts today is not the same peace of the Prince of Peace.

The Prophet Haggai has an interesting comment in the promise given to him by God. Haggai says that there will one day be a peace, and the prophet gives the indicator of when that peace will come. Remember Haggai was a prophet contemporary with Zechariah. They both were prophesying during the time that Zerubbabel was rebuilding the temple, having just returned from the Babylonian captivity.

As Haggai was encouraging the people to help Zerubbabel rebuild the temple, he tells them the *"glory of this latter house shall be greater than the former, saith the Lord of hosts: and in this place will I give peace, saith the Lord of hosts"* (Haggai 2:9). There is a double meaning in Haggai's statement. The prophet is not just speaking about the temple they were building then, but was also looking toward the temple that will be built for Jesus to reign from in the millennial kingdom.

There will be a peace when the Prince of Peace rules in Jerusalem from the temple, the latter house, and it will be so much more magnificent than the former house. The Messiah's Temple will be the one where Jesus Christ will sit on His throne, in the "Holy of Holies." It is from there He will rule and reign over this earth. At that time, Jesus will establish the "real peace."

Many times I have heard the phrase, "Pray for the peace of Jerusalem." Psalm 122:6 says, *"Pray for the peace of Jerusalem: they shall prosper that love thee."*

When a person prays for peace in Jerusalem, they are actually praying for the Prince of Peace to return, since He is the one with the true peace for Jerusalem. What that phrase quoted in Psalms actually means is to pray for the Messiah to return to set up His kingdom with "real peace."

The False Peace

There has been much effort over the years to establish peace. There were the Camp David Accords in 1979, the Oslo Accords in 1993, and the peace agreement between Israel and Jordan in 1994. There is even an attempt for peace between Israel and Syria. There is an ongoing peace effort throughout the entire Middle East region, with leaders from around the world working toward anticipated peace.

Daniel 9:27 relates to us that there will be a peace, howbeit for a short period of time, soon after the Rapture of the Church. Daniel says the Antichrist will confirm a peace agreement with Israel and many other countries for a seven-year period of time. This seven-year period of time does not begin until there has been a peace agreement established between the Antichrist and Israel.

The Rapture could take place days, months, even years before that agreement is confirmed. What we see unfolding in these different attempts for peace with the Egyptians, Syrians, Jordanians, and the Palestinians is "human effort" to bring about that which only the Messiah can install on the earth.

As I looked at the Scripture in Daniel's prophecy about the coming peace treaty between the Antichrist and Israel, I noticed what the Bible does *not* say. It does not say that the Antichrist will "sign" a peace agreement with Israel in that prophecy. What it says is that the Antichrist will "confirm" a peace treaty with Israel. The Hebrew word used in Daniel 9:27 for confirm is "gabar," which translated means strengthen, make stronger, or confirm.

In order to strengthen something, make it stronger, or to confirm it, it must already be there, on the table. In other words, the Antichrist will come and confirm, strengthen, or make stronger a peace agreement, or agreements, that are already on the table but are not really working for the parties. That is exactly the situation we have today. There are peace agreements between Israel and its Arab neighbors on the table, but they are not working as planned.

Chapter 13
The Camp David Accords

In 1966 I was Vice President and General Manager of Olivia Broadcasting Company, which operated WPAX Radio in Thomasville, Georgia. I was invited to meet with a little-known candidate from Plains, Georgia who was running for Governor. I drove to a Holiday Inn on Highway 319 in Thomasville to meet with this young man, Jimmy Carter.

As he started to talk, he spoke to me about his plans and his goals, his desires, and his campaign issues as they related to the governorship of the state of Georgia. Having heard that he was a born-again Christian, I asked him to give me his personal testimony of how Jesus Christ had become his Saviour. He shared his testimony and I was impressed with his love for the Lord. Though not necessarily excited about his politics, because our views differed in a few areas, I was talking with a man who, unknown to both of us then, would not only become Governor of Georgia, but President of the United States, as well. Even more interesting was the fact that he would be involved in the beginning of the peace process between Israel and her Arab neighbors.

After being elected president in 1976, Jimmy Carter made moves in the foreign policy area of his presidency that were not very successful. It was when he got involved in the Middle East that it seemed that the Lord would bring things together for him. Being a "man of the Book," the Bible, he knew well the problems over the centuries which had confronted Israel and its neighbors. This knowledge of the Scriptures gave insight to assist President Carter as he worked to bring

Israel and Egypt to the peace table at his presidential retreat, Camp David.

The Camp David Accords were the product of bold gambles and creative political strategies by President Jimmy Carter, Israeli Prime Minister Menachem Begin, and—most of all—Egyptian President Anwar Sadat. To understand the dynamics behind the remarkable meeting of these three men, you must have not only a basic understanding of Arab-Israeli relations, but you must also be able to recognize the intricacies of international politics. As this story unfolds, be mindful of God's presence on the world scene and observe how these personalities unwittingly set the stage for the future peace treaty foretold in Daniel 9.

Egypt's Search For Peace

This story begins at the end of World War II. Egypt was in the grip of British colonialism. Although a constitutional monarchy was established in 1922, Egypt had only limited autonomy and still very much felt the influence of Britain. The governmental interference exercised by Britain was a sore point for Egyptian nationals. This foreign interference was to affect the personalities of future Egyptian leaders, whose decisions were often based on Egyptian nationalism.

In 1948 Egypt played a major role in the Arab effort to eradicate the newly established state of Israel. Egypt's position on Israel's southern border made them a key player in the 1948 war (and every war thereafter, until 1973). Egypt, as well as the rest of the Arab nations, suffered an overwhelming defeat at the hands of the young nation. As the war was drawing to a close, Israeli forces managed to trap three Egyptian battalions in a group of Arab villages that became known as the Faluja Pocket. One of the soldiers trapped was none other than Colonel Gamal Abdel Nasser, the man who would later become President of Egypt.

Gamal Nasser

Gamal Nasser was born in 1918 to parents of modest means in Alexandria, Egypt. Nasser was raised in a very anti-British environment and even bore a lifelong scar on his forehead as a result of an anti-British street demonstration. After graduating from the Royal Military Academy, Nasser ended up serving in Sudan. While in Sudan, Nasser formed a secret alliance with several other officers, one of whom was Anwar Sadat.

This alliance, called the Free Officers, had as its goal the expulsion of the British and the toppling of the Egyptian monarchy from power. In 1952, Nasser orchestrated what amounted to a bloodless coup. Nasser remained in the background and placed General Mohammad Naguib as his puppet head of state. Within a year, he deposed Naguib and assumed control on his own. In that same year a member of the Muslim Brotherhood, an Islamic fundamentalist terrorist organization, attempted to assassinate Nasser. Nasser angrily pursued the destruction of the Muslim Brotherhood for their act of aggression.

In 1955, Nasser signed an arms agreement with Czechoslovakia, which in effect gave the Soviet Union a foothold in the Middle East. In 1956, Nasser nationalized the Suez Canal in response to the withdrawal of promised support for the Aswan High Dam Project by Britain, France, and the United States. This move, and a series of other events, eventually led to a conflict between Egypt and the combined forces of Britain, France, and Israel.

In the Suez Canal War, these countries gained control over the Suez Canal but were eventually forced to give it back because of the lack of United States support for its allies. Israel was also pressured into giving up all the territorial gains it won in this war. As a result of the Suez Canal War, Britain and France lost most of their influence in the Middle East, the United States became the strongest outside player in the region, and Nasser became a hero in the Arab world.

Nasser, defeated militarily, was victorious in retaining the canal. Because he was perceived as taking on the Western powers and coming out the winner, Nasser was granted a level of prestige unparalleled in the Arab world.

Over the next decade Nasser sought to expand his influence in the Arab world. He created the United Arab Republic with hopes of installing himself as the leader of an alliance of Arab Nations. This initiative stalled, however, and he found himself being pushed to the brink of a war that he did not really want.

In the mid 1960s, Palestinian guerrillas increased the intensity of their raids into Israel. Syria took the opportunity to enhance its position in Arab opinion by openly supporting these Palestinians. In 1966, Israel reacted to the guerrilla raids by conducting a minor military strike into Jordan. Arab sentiments toward Israel worsened.

Up to this point, Egypt's borders were patrolled by the United Nations Emergency Force (UNEF), but now the Arab world began to see Nasser as hiding in weakness behind the UNEF. Nasser asked the UNEF to vacate the area and Egypt began a military buildup along the border. Israel interpreted this as an act of war. On June 5, 1967, Israel conducted a preemptive strike on her Arab neighbors. With brilliant strategic planning and a superior fighting force, Israel scored a stunning success over Egypt, Jordan, and Syria in what became known as the Six-Day War.

This loss was extremely damaging to Nasser. Because of Egypt's vastly superior numbers, popular opinion was that this should have been the war that finally crushed Israel. A thoroughly defeated Nasser submitted his presidential resignation to the Egyptian people. They refused it and allowed him to remain in office, but his effectiveness in politics had been destroyed in the war.

Nasser died just three years later and was succeeded by his vice president, Anwar Sadat. Sadat, too, had been a member of the Free Officers, the military regime that had brought Nasser to power. Many saw Sadat as being a transitional leader until a new government was formed, but he showed his political mettle by surviving a takeover attempt in 1971 and entrenching himself firmly into the presidency.

Anwar Sadat

With his position secure, Sadat began the overwhelming task of bolstering Egypt's economy in the wake of a costly and demoralizing war with Israel. He turned to the Soviets, whom Nasser had fostered a relationship with, and requested more military and economic aid. When none was granted, Sadat expelled the Soviets from Egypt and broke off ties with Moscow. This was the type of stunning move that was to typify the way he did things in the future.

This flair for drama was to manifest itself again in the form of yet another Arab-Israeli war. Sadat joined forces with Syria to secretly plan a surprise attack on Israel in 1973. This attack took place on Israel's holiest day of the year, Yom Kippur, the Day of Atonement. Initially, Syria and especially Egypt experienced remarkable success and rapid advancement into Israeli territory. Sadat's military plan caught Israel totally unprepared and it was easily the most successfully executed attack on Israel by an Arab leader.

After the opening gains, however, Israel recovered and successfully repelled the invaders. In fact, before a cease-fire was negotiated, Israeli forces had pushed forward to within twenty-four miles of the Syrian capital of Damascus and forty-five miles of Cairo, Egypt.

However, Sadat emerged from the Yom Kippur War as an Arab hero. His modest success greatly increased his stature in Egypt. Even in defeat, this war was considered a success because the Arab leaders had not entered it expecting to win. They had wanted to restore Arab pride and bolster their position in the negotiations for a solution to the Palestinian question. Ironically, going to war now allowed Sadat to begin a peace initiative with Israel.

Sadat's Quest For Peace

Sadat immediately began rebuilding towns along the border in an attempt to show that Egypt was through making war with its neighbors. Sadat called for a hasty peace conference in Geneva and welcomed U.S. Secretary of State Henry Kissinger to the Middle East to begin shuttle diplomacy. Despite Sadat's efforts, this peace initiative failed and, to make matters worse, Egypt began experiencing deep economic problems. With the election of the supposedly hawkish Menachem Begin to the post of Israeli Prime Minister, Sadat's hope for peace seemed all but hopeless.

The time had come for Sadat to perform another one of his startling gambles. In a speech delivered on November 9, 1977, to the Egyptian parliament, Sadat declared: "There is no time to lose. I am ready to go to the ends of the earth if that will save one of my soldiers, one of my officers, from being scratched. I am ready to go to their house, to the Knesset, to discuss peace with the Israeli leaders."

At first this statement was not taken seriously by anyone, but when Sadat announced again to CBS-TV's Walter Cronkite that he was willing to go to Israel if asked, it sparked a fierce storm of criticism in the Arab world. No Arab leader had ever even acknowledged Israel's right to exist, much less agreed to negotiate with them in person. Up to that point, all communication between Israeli and Arab counterparts had taken place by way of a mediator. Israeli and Arab representatives had never even stayed in the same hotels when these talks were taking place and now the leader of a major Arab Republic was offering to journey into the midst of the enemy.

This was indeed a bold gamble. Sadat's proposal was promptly accepted by Menachem Begin and on November 19, 1977, Sadat made the 28-minute flight to Jerusalem to address the Israeli Knesset (parliament). In his speech, Sadat explained what he felt were requirements for peace. These requirements were the traditional Arab demands that Israel return all the land captured in the Six-Day War and create a homeland for displaced Palestinians.

This old rhetoric was expected. What was not expected was Sadat's relatively warm words of acceptance for Israel's right to exist as a sovereign nation in the Middle East. Sadat's historic visit laid the groundwork for what was to be the first peace treaty in modern Arab-Israeli history.

As a result of his journey, Sadat was castigated in the Arab world. High officials in Syria, Lebanon, and Iraq immediately called for his assassination. His preferred and only option was to continue what he had started and establish peace with Israel. Egypt's domestic situation was worsening, and he needed the support and legitimacy that the peace agreement would bring from the Western powers, namely the United States. Sadat quickly began to nurture relationships with the two men whose help he would need to pull off this miracle—Jimmy Carter and Menachem Begin.

Jimmy Carter

The accounts of how Carter and Begin came to play their respective roles on the world's stage are every bit as fascinating as Sadat's. Jimmy Carter was a Georgia peanut farmer who had tirelessly worked to become the President of the United States. Although he did not prove to be the shrewdest of politicians, Carter was renowned for his honesty and penchant for fairness.

A champion of human rights, Carter had tried in the past to bring an end to the armed conflict in the Middle East but had never experienced any success. He met personally with several Arab leaders and could never convince any of them, except for Sadat, to deal with Israel. Carter and Sadat struck up a sort of friendship that Sadat was to call upon after his visit to Jerusalem. In a phone call, Carter urged Begin to be careful with comments he might make about Sadat because of Sadat's precarious position in the Arab world. The easy friendship that Carter fostered with these two adversaries was to be crucial later on during the peace talks.

Menachem Begin

Menachem Begin began his ascent to power from modest roots in war-torn Poland. He joined the Zionist movement after graduating from Warsaw University and helped thousands of youth immigrate to Poland. At the outbreak of World War II, Begin escaped from Warsaw, joined the Polish Army, and eventually made his way to Israel. Upon his release from the army, Begin became the Commander of a shadowy organization called the Irgun that fought against the British.

The Irgun also fought to protect young Israel from the Arab forces and Begin became somewhat infamous among the Palestinians for his prowess. Over the next thirty years, Begin rose in rank as a member of the right-wing Likud party that he himself helped to found. When the Likud finally won the elections in 1977, Begin was appointed Prime Minister. Although many felt that his presence would be a deterrent to peace, others felt that a Begin-backed peace would be more likely to include the necessary security needed for public approval.

An Unlikely Trio

And so this unlikely trio of men conspired to do the impossible, bring peace to centuries-old enemies. Carter invited Begin and Sadat to the Presidential Retreat in Camp David, Maryland. Carter describes the mood at the camp in his book, *Keeping Faith*. He explains that although there was really no compatibility between them, both men were very religious and saw themselves as men of destiny.

Carter says it was as if Sadat had "inherited the mantle of authority from the great pharaohs," and that Begin was "cast in a Biblical role as one charged with the future of God's chosen people." Carter kept the media away from Camp David, a move that paid off in allowing the two men to negotiate without the intense scrutiny that usually accompanies such talks. The men debated over points concerning the Israeli withdrawal from the Sinai, the Palestinian issue in Israel, and the manner in which normalization of a future treaty would take place.

The result of these intense meetings was the *Framework for Peace in the Middle East*, a signed document that would directly result in the signing of a full peace treaty on March 26, 1979. Among the items that the treaty addressed was the withdrawal of Israeli armed forces and civilians from Sinai within three years, special security arrangements in Sinai, a buffer zone along the Sinai-Israel border to be manned by United Nations peace-keeping forces, the exchange of ambassadors, and the establishment of normal economic and cultural relations. The question of a Palestinian homeland was to be negotiated later.

This was to be the first peace treaty between Israel and any of her Arab neighbors. Over the years, the promise that this historical event inspired has dimmed somewhat because the full normalization of the treaty has never taken place. Sadat's bold gamble did not bolster Egypt's ailing economy. It was later shown that he, in effect, signed his own death warrant when he signed the treaty. A fringe Muslim group assassinated Anwar Sadat in 1981 for his recognition of Israel. Egypt's new President, Hosni Mubarak, has taken a far more moderate stance in his dealings with the Israelis.

A Treaty Not Working

Though the Camp David Accords has been in effect since 1979, over these many years there has never been a normalization of the agreement between Israel and Egypt. In fact, President Mubarak who was Vice President at the time of the signing of this peace treaty has never officially visited Israel. Egypt's foreign minister has visited Israel and the two countries have exchanged diplomats, but no official leader of Egypt has been to Israel.

There is one exception to that statement. Mubarak did visit Israel in November 1995 at the death of Prime Minister Yitzhak Rabin. Leaders from nations all over the world came to the funeral services. However, when President Mubarak arrived in Israel, he issued a statement that it was not an official visit. He made it clear that he was in Israel for the purpose of honoring Yitzhak Rabin, and he wanted the media to take note that this was the only reason he was in Israel.

The normalization process, which should take place between two nations who have signed a peace treaty, has never come about for Israel and Egypt. Though the two nations live somewhat peacefully in the region today, there is still a "cold peace" between these neighbors. Thus, anticipation for peace, in spite of a valiant effort by both Israel and Egypt, has faltered. What these countries need is for someone to come on the scene and strengthen their agreement; someone needs to *"confirm"* the peace agreement (Daniel 9:27).

Chapter 14
The Oslo Accords

Judy and I had been invited to join other international journalists at the Government Press Office in Jerusalem, on September 13, 1993, to witness an historic event. At approximately 4 p.m., we were ushered into a special room that had been set up with a large screen television, feeding a live satellite picture from the White House in Washington, D.C. We sat watching the broadcast with the other journalists as Bill Clinton, President of the United States, stepped from his office onto the White House lawn. Yitzhak Rabin, Prime Minister of Israel, accompanied the President on one side; Yasser Arafat, Chairman for the Palestinian Liberation Organization, was on the other.

We watched with interest these two foreign leaders who were oddly similar. One had been a military hero with the Israeli Defense Force; a "fighter for freedom." The other, some might also term a "freedom fighter," but his mission was to eliminate the state of Israel and remove the Jewish presence from the Middle East. And both had a common pursuit. Rabin and Arafat were each leading a people who lay claim to the same geographical area in the Middle East.

Arafat had grown up with a deep desire to rid the world of the "Jewish problem." In fact, Arafat has a plan for this to come about, according to the Palestinian Covenant, which he was responsible for helping put together. This Palestinian "constitution" calls for the demise of the state of Israel and the dispersion of the Jewish people to some place outside of the Middle East.

These three men walked across the White House lawn together on that Monday afternoon to be a part of this important meeting, the signing of the Oslo Accords. As we sat there watching this event unfold before our eyes, we all were totally taken aback by the historic significance that it held.

Forming The Oslo Accords

The facts behind this story had been developing for some months, certainly before this meeting at the White House that day. In fact, the story of the Oslo Accords had been coming together since the election of Yitzhak Rabin as Prime Minister of Israel. Rabin's Foreign Minister Shimon Peres, Rabin's number one political rival throughout the years in the Labor Party, was the "architect" behind the Oslo Accords. It was Peres who would actually lay out the plan for the world to see.

Yitzhak Rabin had been chosen to be the candidate for Prime Minister, representing the Labor Party in the 1992 election. His selection was attributed to his military background, his popularity among the Israeli people, and the fact that voters thought that he would be a conservative leader holding firm to the political issues that were so dear to the hearts of the people of Israel.

Those "conservative political issues" could basically be stated as the sovereignty of the Jewish people over the geographical locations that had been won during the wars of Israel. Those wars include the War of Independence (1948), the Six-Day War (1967), the Yom Kippur War (1973), and every other military confrontation since that time.

It was these two men, Rabin and Peres, who would share the Nobel Peace prize with an unlikely partner, Yasser Arafat, because of what was being made public to the world from the White House. What actually happened and the reason for the name "Oslo Accords" was because of the participation of the government of Norway. In addition, there were two Palestinian representatives and two Israeli representatives who met in Oslo to put together this accord.

The Real Story

The real story behind the Oslo Accords is quite fascinating. Yasser Arafat and the PLO were on their last leg going into 1993. They were in danger of losing support at home and throughout the Arab world. At home, Arafat was in grave danger of losing the self-proclaimed title of Palestinian spokesperson to the Islamic fundamentalist group Hamas.

In most of the Arab world, Arafat was in disfavor for siding with Iraq in the Gulf War. This had brought about a serious loss of financial support for the PLO. This loss, combined with the fact that he had not made any progress in peace talks with a supposedly friendly Labor Party, at that time the ruling party in Israel, put Arafat into trouble.

With nothing to lose, Arafat decided to try to secretly work out a deal with Israel. In arranging for the talks to take place, Arafat called on Norwegian Foreign Minister Johan Jorgen Holst. Holst was chosen for the relationship he had fostered between both Arafat and the Labor Party in Israel. Norway was eager to help and Holst quickly offered his country's hospitality.

On January 19, 1993, the Israeli Parliament voted to authorize contacts between Israeli and PLO negotiators. Because of the hard-line stance that most Palestinian leaders took against even recognizing Israel's right to exist, Arafat had to be very careful who he let know about the secret contacts in Oslo. He chose two of his most moderate diplomats as the negotiators and sent them to Oslo along with Israel's contingent from the Foreign Ministry.

The first meetings in February and April took place at the Hotel Plaza in Oslo, as well as Holst's private farm in the village of Borregaard. The Israeli position was that they would offer autonomy in the Gaza Strip while the Palestinians claimed, at Arafat's urging, that they needed some sort of concession in the West Bank region as well. The Palestinian negotiators then came up with what they called the "Leopard Spot" plan.

This "Leopard Spot" plan advocated that Israel begin to allow autonomy in certain West Bank cities, which were basically populated only by Arabs. It was called the "Leopard Spot" plan because a map of the West Bank which displayed Palestinian autonomous areas around cities like Nablus, Bethlehem, Ramallah, and Jericho, had spots like you would find on a leopard.

Israel showed a willingness to work with this plan but there were still several problems that had to be worked out. The Israelis insisted that there be provisions, which would allow for Israel to work with Arafat on apprehending Palestinian terrorists. They also demanded that Arafat change the portion of the Palestinian National Covenant that called for Israel's destruction. Arafat was to agree to these concessions, but it is up for debate as to whether he has ever come through with his part of the bargain.

A Difficult Peace

The main sticking point in the agreement that was to become the Oslo Accords was the fate of eastern Jerusalem, which the Palestinians felt should be their capital in a Palestinian state called Palestine. In order to make a deal, both sides decided to put this question on hold until a later date. The discussion on Jerusalem would take place during the final status talks, along with the questions on the return of Palestinian refugees, the disposition of the Jewish settlements, and the release of Palestinian prisoners.

After the basic tenants of the Oslo Accords were drawn up, it was only a matter of time before the negotiators hammered out the final arrangements. After eleven more meetings in Norway, the agreement was approved in principle when Peres visited Oslo on August 19-20. The final document would actually be only a shell of the ultimate agreement. This was the main problem with the Oslo Accords, it was only a document that was meant to be a starting point for the two parties, they would have to negotiate their way to a truly "final agreement."

The secret meetings between the two representatives from both the Palestinians and Israelis had taken place in Oslo, Norway, under the leadership of Shimon Peres, with the approval of Yitzhak Rabin, then Israeli Prime Minister. However, there were many problems in the Israeli delegation. Even at the time of the signing of the accord at the White House, there was tension between Peres and Rabin because Peres was jealous of Rabin taking the center stage.

Another problem, just before the signing ceremony, was that Yasser Arafat, dressed in his military uniform, wanted to carry his revolver throughout the White House. White House security would not allow this, but he did show up at the peace-signing ceremony wearing his military uniform when everyone else was wearing dress suits. Dressed as he was, Arafat made a statement to the world that if he were not able to use the negotiating table to achieve his desires and goals, he would then revert to military action to accomplish them.

The Palestinian Covenant

Yasser Arafat gave strong evidence that he had no intention of normalizing a peace agreement with Israel, even though he signed the Oslo Accords. I have a copy of a letter in my file from Yasser Arafat to Yitzhak Rabin dated four days before the signing of the Oslo Accords on the White House lawn on September 13, 1993. The letter states that Arafat would remove the questionable clauses in the Palestinian Covenant.

The Palestinian Covenant is a constitution for the Palestinian people. It is the written statement for their efforts to gain a homeland; a state with Jerusalem as its capital. In the covenant there are over thirty clauses that call for the elimination of the Jewish people and the removal of the Jewish state from the Middle East. This document was supposed to be changed, according to a letter Arafat wrote to Rabin before they both signed the Oslo Accords at the White House.

However, as I sit writing this book, these clauses are still in the Palestinian Covenant. They have not been removed during the seven years following the signing of the accords and there are those who say that there were never really any plans by the Palestinians for removing these clauses from the Palestinian Covenant.

The Historic Signing

President Bill Clinton, Israeli Prime Minister Yitzhak Rabin, and PLO Chairman Yasser Arafat sat at a very historic table on the stage on the White House lawn that day. They signed the document, the Oslo Accords, and then as the three stood there, Bill Clinton put his hand on Rabin's back and pushed him toward Yasser Arafat, literally forcing the two men to shake hands. Arafat was a sworn enemy of the Jews, an international terrorist who had killed many Jewish people around the world. But now, here he was shaking hands with an Israeli military hero—the Prime Minister of Israel.

It has been said that Arafat has more Jewish blood on his hands than any man since Hitler. It is documented that he also has more Palestinian blood on his hands than any man in history. Arafat has called for the assassination of many Palestinian people who collaborated with the Jewish people or the Israeli government. He has also called for the death penalty for any Palestinian who sells his land to Jewish people.

As Rabin and Arafat shook hands, the journalists who had gathered in the press office in Jerusalem gasped out loud. In absolute dismay, they could not believe what they had just seen on satellite television. When the ceremony was over and Judy and I were driving back to our apartment, we were almost run off the road by a car full of Palestinian teenagers. Hanging out of their windows, they shouted and waved Palestinian flags. The actions of these Palestinian young people indicated that they believed this was the event in history that would now give them the right to establish a Palestinian state in the country of Israel.

An Unresolved Treaty

The Oslo Accords stipulated that there would be no unilateral naming of a state, and there would be no flag representing a Palestinian state on display. These stipulations, found both in the accords and all other agreements signed by the two parties since 1993, have been overlooked by the Palestinians. As you travel in any of the autonomous areas under the Palestinian Authority in Gaza, Jericho, or the West Bank, you will see the Palestinian "flag" flying on roof tops, from poles, and from government buildings.

As we have seen since this document was signed, there have been many problems with the Oslo Accords. Many say that the Oslo Accords were doomed from the very outset. In fact, one of the main reasons for this was that consideration was not given to the security needs of the Jewish people in the state of Israel. That happened because there were no security officials or military personnel involved in the negotiations that were held in Oslo, Norway.

Since the Oslo Accords were signed, there has been a breakdown on both sides to abide by the agreement. In the final analysis, most of the failure to abide by the dictates of the agreement comes from the Palestinian side. One example is that they never removed the clauses from the Palestinian Covenant calling for the destruction of the Jewish state.

Another example is the directive that calls for only 18,000 Palestinian police to serve as a policing unit to govern the Palestinian areas. Today there are over 50,000 Palestinian policemen who serve and they have actually become a military force for Arafat. At times, the weapons that were issued by the Israeli government for this police force have been turned on the Israeli people, some of them even used in terrorist attacks.

There have been more terrorist attacks and more Jewish people killed since the Oslo Accords were signed in September 1993 than there were from the establishment of the state of Israel, in 1948, until 1993. This is continuing evidence that the Oslo Accords are not being normalized. This makes a second peace agreement between Israel and the Arab people that is not being normalized.

The final status talks had to deal with some very tough issues like the sovereignty of Jerusalem, the statehood of the Palestinian people, and the return of the Palestinian Diaspora, those Palestinians who had been scattered across the world who would like to come back into Israel. There is also the situation of the Jewish settlements across Israel on the table. The question must be resolved as to whether they will become a part of the new Palestinian Authority or state, or whether they will stay under Israel.

Even with some kind of an agreement between the Israelis and the Palestinians over these major issues discussed in the final status talks, the Oslo Accords have failed and there are many unsolved problems still remaining. Just signing a piece of paper will not bring together two peoples who have hated each other for years, and even centuries. The record shows that there have been infractions of the rules in the Oslo Accords on both sides. What this agreement needs is for someone to come and strengthen it; make it stronger. Someone needs to *"confirm"* the peace agreement (Daniel 9:27).

Chapter 15
The Israeli-Jordanian Peace Agreement

As I stood in the sands of the Arabah, the extension of the Jordan Valley from the Dead Sea south to the Red Sea, I realized that I was going to witness history in the making. The Arabah, located just north of Eilat, the southernmost city in Israel on the Red Sea, would host this historic event. I stood on that desert site witnessing Jordan's King Hussein, and all of his political leaders, come together with Israel's Prime Minister Yitzhak Rabin, and all of his political leaders.

United States President Bill Clinton, accompanied by Secretary of State Warren Christopher, made his way to the platform to finalize the Israeli-Jordanian Peace Agreement. At the press briefing from the director of the Government Press Office the night before in Eilat, they told us that this was to be staged for the large gathering of journalists who were there to witness this historic event.

An Historic Event

The director's statements would be true, as we were to find out. The next day we were taken out to the site of the signing in air-conditioned buses, passing through security with no check at all, and ushered into our area just in front of the temporary stage erected for the signing of this peace agreement. Prominent newscasters from throughout the world had been sent to cover this event. I noticed Peter Jennings of ABC, Tom Brokaw of NBC, Connie Chung of CBS; all of the CNN reporters were there, as well. In all, over one thousand journalists were gathered for this historic event.

This was going to be the climax of overtures that had been taking place through the years to develop a peace between Israel and Jordan. The border between Israel and Jordan is the longest border that Israel shares with any of its Arab neighbors, motivating an effort by both sides to try and achieve a meaningful peace.

These efforts date back as far as King Abdullah, King Hussein's grandfather and the present Jordanian King's namesake and great grandfather. King Abdullah I endeavored to come to a peace agreement when he held secret meetings with Golda Meir, who was then a member of the Israeli cabinet. In fact, it is reported that the assassination of King Abdullah was for the purpose of stopping any peace effort between Israel and Jordan.

The assassination of King Abdullah took place on the Temple Mount in Jerusalem just outside the El Aksa Mosque, when a Palestinian young person took a pistol and shot the king of Jordan at point-blank range. The young man said he killed the king because Abdullah was trying to make peace with the Israeli people.

News reports prior to the peace treaty signing between Israel and Jordan indicated that Yitzhak Rabin had been meeting secretly with King Hussein and was trying to put something together even before they made public the peace efforts that were going on between the two countries.

In fact, the first public mention of the peace effort came on July 25, 1994, when U.S. President Bill Clinton invited Israeli Prime Minister Yitzhak Rabin and Jordan's King Hussein to meet with him at the White House. It was then that they announced to the world the Declaration of Principles, which was the precursor for the peace agreement that would finally be drawn up.

Jordan's Custodial Rights

During that announcement at the White House, President Bill Clinton announced to the world that King Hussein would be named the custodian of the Islamic holy sites in Jerusalem. These sites include the Dome of the Rock, the El Aksa Mosque, and the Cave of the Patriarchs (located at Hebron); plus other locations that Islamics claim as holy sites in the land of Israel. King Hussein had to be named the custodian of these Islamic holy sites in any agreement that was made, because that was the only authority upon which his monarchy could exist.

Tradition has it that King Hussein's family dates back to Mohammad and that his great-great-grandfather was the sherif of Mecca and Medina, which meant that he was the custodian of those holy sites for the Islamic faith. This was the basis upon which King Abdullah was able to establish a monarchy in Jordan. Now it was a reason for the documentation of the monarchy of King Hussein in Jordan.

After hearing this announcement, Yasser Arafat became livid about the President's statements. He realized that the only way he could pursue his goal of having Jerusalem as the capital of a Palestinian state was to have sovereignty over the holy sites and to be the sole representative of the Palestinian people in Israel. Because of President Clinton's announcement, Arafat shunned the treaty signing ceremony.

The Israeli-Jordanian Treaty

A very historical event unfolded that day,

October 26, 1994. As I stood, just yards away from the platform where all of the activities were taking place, I noticed the politicos that had gathered from Jordan and Israel, and the entourage from the United States. I realized that this history-making event was telling the world that another Arab nation was going to make peace with the Jewish people.

Although the first two peace agreements, the Camp David Accords and the Oslo Accords, did not seem to be normalizing, there were great prospects for this particular peace agreement. There were many aspects of this agreement that would benefit both the Israelis and the Jordanians. In addition, both of these countries and their leadership had been working for years to make this happen.

Looking at my copy of this peace agreement, I noticed several directives of the treaty that would help the two nations normalize their relations. For example, Article 13, which is titled "Transportation and Roads," took note of the progress already made in the area of transportation. The parties recognized the mutuality of this interest and the need for good neighborly relations in the area of transportation and agreed to promote relations between them in this sphere.

The treaty stated: "Each party will permit the free movement of nationals and vehicles of the other into and within its territory according to the general rules applicable to nationals and vehicles of other states." This interesting phrase stated that they were going to exchange opportunities of transportation between the two states, that the borders would be open. Further: "The Parties will open and maintain roads and border-crossings between their countries and will consider further road and rail links between them."

The King's Highway

The fourth and last point in the article says: "The Parties agree to continue their negotiations for a highway to be constructed and maintained between Egypt, Israel and Jordan near Eilat." What an interesting thought, simply catching my eye and taking me back to Isaiah 19:23 which says, *"In that day shall there be a highway out of Egypt to Assyria"* (today's Syria).

Prophetically this highway will open up opportunities to Syria and Egypt and Israel to come together to worship in the Temple Mount in Jerusalem during the millennium. This highway is also referred to in Numbers 20:17 as the *"kings high way;"* a highway that will extend from Egypt in the south through Israel and Jordan and up into Syria. In the peace treaty between Israel and Jordan, the documentation of the peace agreement calls for the construction of the highway to be a joint project between Israel and Jordan.

The Petra Factor

One of the most exciting things about this peace agreement, in addition to the fact that there was going to be peaceful coexistence between these two peoples, is Article 17. It says: "The Parties affirm their mutual desire to promote co-operation between them in the field of tourism. In order to accomplish this goal, the Parties—taking note of the understandings reached between them concerning tourism—agree to negotiate as soon as possible...."

They were to conclude, not later than three months from the exchange of the instrument for the ratification of this treaty, with an agreement to facilitate and encourage mutual tourism and tourism from third party countries. It was an unbelievable article; one that allowed the Jewish people to become tourists in Jordan and, vice versa, for the Jordanian people to visit Israel. What a breakthrough Article 17 was allowing to take place.

We put a man on the street right after this peace agreement was signed and we asked the question, "What is the most significant result of the peace agreement?" Overwhelmingly, ninety-six percent of the people responded that the most important result of this peace agreement was that they could now have the opportunity to visit Petra. This has great prophetic significance.

Many Bible teachers conclude that Petra is the place, prepared by God, where He will house one-third of the Jewish people during the terrible "time of Jacob's trouble" in the last three-and-a-half years of the Tribulation Period. For many years prior to this peace agreement, when passage was forbidden, there was a desire among young Jewish men to sneak across the border to Petra and return, proving their manhood at having been able to break this border. Now, an official government document allows the Jewish people to freely travel to Petra, before the Tribulation, so that they can become familiar with the location where God will house them.

The Jerusalem Post also conducted a poll, asking people when they would like to visit Petra. They answered that they wished they could visit it that day. Over the years since this agreement was signed, numerous Jews have made their way as tourists into Petra.

A Prophetic Treaty

Many provisions in this peace agreement draw parallels to prophecies laid out in God's Word. Just the fact that there is a peace agreement between Israel and Jordan allows for the prophetic scenario of Daniel 11 to be fulfilled. In Daniel 11, the Antichrist comes into the Middle East and goes to the north, defeating Syria, then turns to the south, defeating Egypt. On his way south, he goes through Edom, Moab, and the chief of the children of Ammon (modern-day Jordan)—but he doesn't touch it. I believe the Antichrist spares Jordan because God will preserve this area to protect His people in Petra in the terrible time of trouble that is ahead.

This peace agreement comes the closest to being normalized of any peace agreement that has been signed by Israel and an Arab nation. However, there are problems that still must be resolved: the allocation of water rights is still in dispute, as well as questions relative to certain items in the document itself.

There is also a segment of the Jordanian society that does not want to even recognize the reality of a Jewish state in the Middle East, much less sign a peace treaty with them. This group of Islamic fundamentalists has been increasing in power and influence among the Jordanian people since the signing of the treaty in 1994. The group, Hamas, which is headquartered in Ammon, is ready to overthrow the present Jordanian leadership, if need be, to accomplish their goal of ridding the Middle East of a Jewish presence.

As we can see, another peace agreement signed by Israel and one of its Arab neighbors is now on the table. Though present problems do not jeopardize the good relations enjoyed by Israel and Jordan, there is that faction in Jordan that is working to undermine the peace treaty. This sets the stage for yet another peace agreement that needs to be strengthened or made stronger—actually *"confirmed"* by a world leader (Daniel 9:27).

Chapter 16
The Search for Peace with Syria

Being a journalist and living in Jerusalem, I sit front row, center stage at the scene where the last act will be performed, where God's prophetic scenario will all unfold. Jerusalem is one of the most populated cities in the world for journalists, second only to Washington, D.C. I have had the opportunity here in Israel to monitor the comments of many world leaders and in particular the leaders of Arab nations surrounding Israel, those nations who have been traditional enemies of the Jewish people.

It is not often that I agree with statements made by these Arab leaders, in light of their determination to remove the Jewish people from the land of Israel, to eliminate the state of Israel, and to expel the Jewish people from the Middle East. But I have to agree with a statement made not long ago by President Assad of Syria. He said that the problem behind the conflict in the Middle East is that the Jewish people believe the Bible and they believe that God has given them all of this land.

Well, that statement I agree with because the Bible does state that all of this land belongs to God—who has promised to give it to the Jewish people in the last days. God promised Abraham the land, which includes borders extending from Cairo, Egypt, in the south, through the Sinai and Gaza Strip, up the coasts of Israel, Lebanon, and Syria, and over to the Euphrates River; extending south and east through Syria and Iraq, following the Euphrates River to the Persian Gulf;

extending south, through Saudi Arabia, to the Red Sea. These boundaries include all of the Sinai Peninsula, all of Lebanon, all of Syria, half of Iraq, half of Saudi Arabia, all of Jordan, plus modern-day Israel.

What God has promised is ten times as much as what Israel has and controls today. Suffice it to say, Israel will only control the other nine-tenths of what God has promised to them during the time of real, true peace in the millennial kingdom to come.

That, of course, is not what President Assad meant. And although he has been a continual thorn in the flesh for the Israelis, there are efforts by both Israel and Syria for peace between these two longtime enemies.

A Search For Peace

It is quite interesting to note that the approach that President Assad has to the peace process is "land for peace." In fact, the first conversation that President Assad had with Benjamin Netanyahu was before he became Prime Minister of Israel. It was back in 1992 at the Madrid Conference, when then Deputy Foreign Minister Netanyahu made a statement to President Assad that if he wanted "peace for land," that would be just fine with Israel. "You give us the Golan Heights and we will guarantee you peace." This was not what President Assad had in mind.

Assad says that they want all of the land of the Golan Heights and, in return, Syria will give Israel peace. By the way, when Assad says "all of the land," he's talking about the land all the way down to the eastern shores of the Sea of Galilee. It is important to note that Syria controlled the Golan Heights from 1948 to 1967, but there was no peace then.

The demands of President Assad for the Golan Heights include all previously controlled land that Syria had under its leadership from 1948 to 1967. This is going to be a burr in the saddle of the settlers as they struggle for security. This struggle is not only for their homes and businesses and families in the Golan Heights, but also for security for the nation of Israel.

As I explained earlier in this book, the Golan Heights is of paramount strategic and political importance to the state of Israel. President Assad's assurance that Israel's surrendering of the Golan Heights will bring about peace does not ring true to the Israelis living in the Galilee region of the country. These are the same citizens who were made to tolerate periodic artillery and tank fire into civilian neighborhoods in the years between 1948 and 1967. That haphazard destruction is what spurred Israel to take control of the Golan Heights in the first place.

Even though General Dayan, the Israeli Defense Minister in 1967, knew the importance of the Golan Heights region, he was very apprehensive about launching an attack against Syria. He worried that if Syria lost ground to Israel, it might bring the Russians into the armed conflict. Eventually, General Dayan was forced into action by the Israelis who had settled in the north. These settlers were tired of the lethal harassment and urged the military to answer Syria attacks by occupying the Heights from which these attacks were taking place. Before General Dayan could do that, he first had to make sure that Israel's southern and eastern fronts were secure. Only when Egypt had been subdued in the Sinai and Jordan had been thrown out of the West Bank did Dayan turn his attention toward Syria and the Golan Heights.

Dayan's Directive

On the morning of June 9, 1967, General Dayan

gave the go-ahead to Major-General David Elazar, the commander of the Northern Front, to take the Golan Heights. The next twenty-four hours were filled with intense fighting on both sides. Among the Israeli soldiers who showed the highest bravery were the members of the infantry force dubbed the "Golani Brigade."

The Golani Brigade was involved in some particularly intense fighting in the foothills of Mount Hermon against firmly entrenched Syrian positions. Against the first position they attacked, the position was captured but only three members of the military unit survived unharmed. In the attack on the second position, the commander of the assault and most of his men sustained serious injuries. Under heavy fire, many of these soldiers threw their bodies on top of the coils of concertina wire, creating a "human bridge" for other soldiers to cross and attack the position.

Similar tales of bravery were repeated all over the Golan Heights as Israel quickly began to push back the Syrian forces. Finally, at mid-morning on June 10, the Syrian military broke down and began to panic. They proceeded to blow up their fortifications and flee before the advancing Israelis. The United Nations finally imposed a cease-fire at 6:30 p.m., but not before Israel had advanced to a strategic point opposite the Damascus plains and had secured safety for the inhabitants of the Golan Heights in the Galilee region. They also set up a buffer zone against future Syrian attacks.

It was at this time that many Israelis moved into the Golan Heights and began the tedious task of building their homes, raising their families, and establishing their businesses in this very fertile area. General Moshe Dayan made the decision to populate this area because now the Golan Heights and those settlers on the Heights would be the first line of defense. They were to make certain that the fifth largest military might of the world, the Syrian military, would not have the opportunity to invade the security of the Jewish people living in northern Israel.

Lebanon's Struggle

Although Israel's capture of the Golan Heights brought safety to the Galilee region in Northern Israel, over the next fifteen years other problems began to develop that eventually required Israeli military intervention. The emergence of the Palestine Liberation Organization (PLO), based in the Bekaa Valley of Lebanon, posed a serious threat to Israel. The PLO not only threatened Israel, but also the Lebanese Christian community.

In an effort to protect themselves from PLO attacks, the Christians requested intervention from the Arab world. An Arab contingent moved into Lebanon to act as a peace-keeping force. One-by-one the other members of the Arab contingency left Lebanon until only Syria remained. Syria's "peace-keeping" force eventually became an "occupying" force of over 30,000 troops intent on making Lebanon a vassal state controlled totally by the Syrian government. Further proof of that fact is that Syria has never recognized Lebanon as an independent country. They consider Lebanon a part of "Greater Syria."

The Christians in Lebanon were now being attacked by both the PLO and the Syrian military. In a last ditch cry for help, they turned to the Israelis to save them from possible annihilation. The peril that the Lebanese Christians were in caused Prime Minister Begin to send the Israeli Air Force into Lebanon where they shot down two Syrian helicopters that were supplying the attacking Syrian forces.

The Israeli and Syrian Armies then began a succession of activities that effectively constituted a buildup in preparation for war. Although a true "hot" war was not to break out between Israel and Syria at this time, the PLO took advantage of the situation and began heavy and indiscriminate gunfire along the Lebanese border into the Northern Galilee region. Israel could not live with this danger to civilian life and soon mounted an attack against the PLO in the Bekaa Valley.

These attacks were disruptive to life in northern Galilee and very damaging to the PLO forces. These circumstances caused both sides to seek a cease-fire and one was finally reached. This cease-fire was not to last long, however, because the reason for the PLO's very existence was to fight Israel, and it found itself losing support at home and in the Arab world.

In order to resume their attacks against Israel, the PLO decided to interpret the cease-fire as applying only to the Lebanese border. They began attacking Israel from the Jordanian border and targeting Israelis traveling abroad. In total, the PLO committed over 240 acts of violence against Israel during the supposed cease-fire.

Operation Peace For Galilee

Finally, on June 6, 1982, Israel decided that, for its own security, it was necessary to create a demilitarized zone north of the Lebanese border. This meant that Israel needed to advance some twenty-five miles into Lebanon to put, as the government spokesperson said, "all settlements in Galilee out of range of terrorist artillery positioned in Lebanon." This maneuver was named "Operation Peace for Galilee."

The removal of the PLO proved to be an arduous task indeed. The PLO had created a state within a state by superseding the Lebanese authority wherever they camped. This created very troublesome conditions for the Lebanese civilians who were forced to do as the PLO commanded or die. Through fierce fighting, the Israeli Defense Force (IDF) slowly began to root out the PLO from southern Lebanon. In many cases the going was slow because the IDF sought to limit the amount of civilian casualties the war produced.

These efforts were made next to impossible by the PLO, who held civilians hostage in order to prevent Israeli attacks. Little-by-little, though, the IDF succeeded in ripping out the PLO infrastructure that was based in southern Lebanon. As the IDF pushed the PLO further into Lebanon, the PLO began to seek shelter by hiding behind the Syrian forces stationed in the 25-mile demilitarized zone.

Israel announced that they would not engage the Syrians unless they themselves were first attacked. Israel passed messages through Washington that suggested that Syria should take control of the PLO and prevent them from shelling Israel. When Syria did not respond to this request and instead began to strengthen its forces along the Israeli-Syrian border, Israel decided to engage Syria. Small skirmishes between the Syrians and the Israelis broke out into full-scale fighting as Israel continued their quest for a 25-mile security zone. The Syrian Air Force began to attack the Israeli forces and soon six Syrian MiG fighters were shot down without any losses on the Israeli side.

When Israel finally decided to push Syria back to twenty-five miles, they realized that the Israeli Air Force was going to have to get heavily involved. In order to safely provide air support for the advancing Israeli troops, Israel was going to have to wipe out the Surface to Air Missiles (SAMs) that Syria had placed in the Bekaa Valley. These SAM batteries were of the same type that had caused so many casualties in the Yom Kippur War and the Syrians were counting on them to keep Israeli Air Force involvement to a minimum.

However, on June 9, the fourth day of fighting, the Israeli Air Force attacked the SAM batteries; they totally destroyed nineteen of them and severely damaged four others without losing a single plane. This attack provoked a strong response from the Syrian Air Force. They launched what was to prove to be the most dramatic dogfights in air warfare history.

One hundred Russian-made MiG fighters from the Syrian Air Force engaged one hundred Israeli fighters in an incredible display of firepower over the Bekaa Valley. When the fighting was finally over, twenty-nine MiGs had been shot down without the loss of a single Israeli plane. This epic battle served to establish total air superiority for the Israelis.

Israel's Victory

With Israel's stunning victory in the air, a Syrian counter-offensive against Israel in the Golan Heights was defused. Many had felt that if Syria became involved militarily with Israel, it might give them the impetus to try and take back the Golan Heights. However, the destruction of the SAMs in the Bekaa Valley, combined with loss of fifteen percent of their Air Force, caused them to think very differently. Israel's total domination of the air, and consequent control of the battle on the ground, even made the officials at the Warsaw Pact headquarters and NATO rethink the balance of power in the Middle East.

With the battle in the air won, Israel's advancement on the ground was only a matter of time. Israeli forces eventually fought all the way to Beirut and surrounded this beleaguered city. The PLO was extremely stubborn and heavy fighting was required to remove them from their strongholds in Lebanon. Finally, in mid July, U.S. Ambassador Phillip Habib began to negotiate for the evacuation of some 6,000 PLO fighters and the remnants of the Syrian troops from Beirut. On July 14, the Lebanese government called for the removal of all foreign military from Lebanese soil. This was the first time that Lebanon had called for this policy, one which not only Israel endorsed, but the United States, as well.

Operation Peace for Galilee was a success for the superior Israeli Defense Force. It was initiated to stop the rocket attacks from the Lebanese border and it effectively did so. Even more, though, it almost totally annihilated the PLO (and it would have if Arafat and the PLO had not been revived by the Oslo Accords) and it established total military dominance over Syria.

The presence of Israeli families in the Golan Heights has helped to maintain peace and security not only for the residents of the Heights, but for all of Israel. There have been, over the years, many moves by the politicians to change the status quo of the situation in the Golan Heights. In particular, United States politicians have applied pressure to Israeli leaders to return the Golan Heights to Syria, for a so-called peace.

Golan Settlers

There is a determination on the part of the settlers there to stay in this area, and not to be removed. Many of the settlers have said that the only way they are going to leave the Golan Heights is in a "body bag." I interviewed one 19-year-old youth who told me he had been born in the Golan Heights and had grown up there with his family. I talked to him about the problems that may come, with Syrian military forces moving in and trying to take by force the Golan Heights. When I asked him how he would respond to that, he told me that the settlers had dug fox holes around their settlement and that they would fight, from these fox holes, any advances made by the Syrians.

Then I asked him what they would do if the Israeli government made a decision to give back the Golan Heights to Syria. Without hesitation, he answered that if the Israeli government came to remove them from their land, they would go into those same fox holes and fight the Israelis. They would fight for the land that they gained back in 1967—whether being taken from them or given away. There is a determination on the part of these settlers and they're ready for a struggle in their hopes of peace and security on the Golan Heights.

For any Israeli leader, it is going to be a tough decision to make. Does the leader give up the land belonging to families and thriving businesses for a piece of paper that has a peace agreement written on it? While this has been under consideration, much political posturing has been taking place. When the late Prime Minister Yitzhak Rabin was alive and negotiating, there were reports that secret negotiations took place between Rabin and Assad. In fact, the Syrians say that Rabin verbally agreed to give back the Golan Heights in order to gain a peace relationship with the Syrian government.

Former Israeli Prime Minister Netanyahu (1996-1999), in an effort to ease strained relations, promoted ongoing discussions between members of his staff and members of Syrian President Assad's staff.

U.S. President Bill Clinton has endeavored throughout his administration to bring about this potential peace between Israel and Syria. Twenty-seven times he has sent Secretary of State Warren Christopher to the Middle East to meet with Assad. Clinton himself even visited President Assad in Damascus in 1994.

Up until now, this peace between Israel and Syria has eluded all parties concerned.

TREND 4

Arrangements

Chapter 17
Arrangements for the Temple

As I sat in my office in New York City, I looked across my desk at one of the most controversial Jewish rabbis in the world. I was about to learn that there was a movement among certain Jews to work at what would be the answer to the prayers of hundreds and thousands of Jewish people over the last two thousand years. That charismatic Jewish leader was Rabbi Meir Kahana and the answer to the prayers of thousands, to rebuild the temple on the Temple Mount in Jerusalem, was the driving force in his life.

I first met Meir Kahana when the rabbi was introduced to me by one of the broadcasters who had a weekly talk program on the radio station I was managing for the Salem Broadcasting Company in New York City. The rabbi was meeting with me to request the opportunity of starting his own weekly talk show on our station. As was my policy, I would spend time with each new broadcaster before we came to a final agreement on the program.

It was at this time that I shared my own personal testimony about my faith in Jesus Christ. I shared with Meir Kahana, an Orthodox Jew, the plan of salvation for not only Jewish people but also for the whole world. The rabbi listened very attentively and then responded with statements that set me back in my seat. Kahana expressed the belief that I was "there for such a time as this," that everything either one of us did must be for the "glory of God" because what God does is for "His holy namesake," and that he had one driving desire.

When I asked the rabbi what that "driving desire" was, his answer caused me to sit upright in my seat. Meir Kahana told me that the driving force in his life was to "build the Third Temple in Jerusalem." I immediately asked him why he wanted to rebuild the temple. His response: "I know that the day the Third Temple is completed, the Messiah will come."

A Third Temple

This mention of a "third temple" by the rabbi was the first time I really started to look into the possibility of the Jewish people moving ahead with the desire of all their prayers. Three times daily there are prayers offered up by those gathering at the Western Wall in Jerusalem: "May our temple be rebuilt in this day here in the holy city."

With this interest in the reconstruction of the ancient Jewish temple in Jerusalem now very real to me, I wanted to know more about the temple. I also wanted to know more about the people involved in the preparations to build the temple. The conversation with Rabbi Kahana had opened a dialogue with one of the key personalities in the preparation process for the Jewish temple.

My investigation into the personalities and the projects involved in the preparations for the temple would bring me into contact with an interesting cast of characters and organizations. In fact, the rabbi's own brother, Nachman Kahana, would come into focus as the philosophical "leader" of this whole modern-day movement.

This interest in rebuilding the temple has been a part of the Jewish fabric down through the centuries, since Herod's Temple was destroyed during the invasion of the City of Jerusalem by General Titus and his Roman Army in 70 A.D. As already mentioned, the daily prayers of the Jewish people are for the rebuilding of the temple to begin immediately. This current activity is the result of years of prayers.

Poking around and asking questions is the way an investigative reporter goes about his business. As I followed this format, I became aware of the intense activity to restore the temple to daily Jewish life. One man, a former member of the Jerusalem city council, has started an organization to get the attention of the Jewish world for the purpose of rebuilding the temple.

The Temple Mount Faithful

That man is Gershon Salomon, who had the unique opportunity of being shown around the Temple Mount several days after the Jewish people had reunited the City of Jerusalem in the Six-Day War in 1967. It was not long afterward that Gershon started the "Temple Mount Faithful." These modern-day zealots formed an organization to encourage the Jewish world to follow the Biblical mandate to once again establish God's house in Jerusalem.

The official Jordanian guide who showed Gershon Salomon around the Temple Mount in June 1967 told him that he believed the Jewish people had come to Jerusalem to rebuild their temple. This guide told Gershon that the Muslims believe the Jews will one day actually restore their worship in Jerusalem by rebuilding their temple on the Temple Mount.

They might have started the process to rebuild the temple in 1967 if the Israeli government had not given control of the Temple Mount to the Jordanians, under an arrangement to appease the Arab world. Today the Temple Mount is administered by an

Islamic trust called the "Waqf." There is a big struggle going on between the Palestinians and the Jordanians as to who actually has the authority to care-take the Temple Mount.

Control Of The Temple Mount

The control of this very sacred piece of real estate, the Temple Mount, and the preparations to build a temple on the spot now occupied by the Dome of the Rock has become the focus of the battle cry of the Arab world. A Jewish temple on the Temple Mount in Jerusalem jeopardizes what they want for the Palestinians, the right to name Jerusalem as the capital of their new state, Palestine.

In fact, in the summer of 1998 the Conference of Islamic Foreign Ministers met in Casablanca under the presidency of Morocco's King Hassan II. It was called to discuss the question of Jerusalem and was viewed as an integral part of an offensive, on all fronts, which the Arabs have launched against Israel. Nothing untoward has occurred in Jerusalem which would necessitate such urgent Islamic action.

At this meeting, Yasser Arafat told the Islamic Foreign Ministers that "Israel has already announced its desire to start a war over the holy City of Jerusalem, and has declared its plans regarding the Holy Temple." Arafat stated, "Israel's sole goal since its conquest of Jerusalem in 1967 has been to 'purify' and 'Judaize' Jerusalem." Arafat added, "Of late, Israel has initiated the great war to make Jerusalem 'Israeli' in order to kill our master, Mohammed."

There will be a major conflict over Jerusalem in the last days, according to the ancient Jewish prophets. However, the Biblical mandate is to build a third temple at the same location of the two previous temples. This mandate has motivated a segment of Orthodox Judaism to actively prepare to start construction on this coming temple.

The Temple Institute

The Temple Institute is a collective of scholars, headed up by Rabbi Israel Ariel, who have studied the Biblical requirements for preparing the priests, the priestly garments, the musical instruments, and the implements for the sacrifices and worship at the temple. These rabbis have commissioned artisans to actually make the items needed to operate the next temple.

For the first time in almost two thousand years there are people busily at work getting things in order to begin services at the Jewish temple in Jerusalem. The personalities involved in the preparations and projects, which must be in place for the operation of the temple, are dedicated to the cause.

This movement is the most outstanding evidence of the soon coming of the Messiah. Though there has been activity to build another temple in Jerusalem over the last two thousand years, there has never been this much progress in the preparations. This is strong evidence of the nearness of the Lord's return.

Chapter 18
Preparations to Become Priests

As I met with Rabbi Nachman Kahana in his yeshiva—a place of learning for Jewish young men—he was working at his computer. He told me he was using the computer to study the Torah, the first five books of the Old Testament. I asked him if he had any other use for his computer, to which he answered in the affirmative. "What?" I asked. He responded, "I have a database on this computer." Of course, my next question was to ask what information was in the database.

His response sent chills up my spine. The rabbi told me that he had on his computer, in the database, the names of all Jewish men in the world who were qualified to be priests. Naturally, my next question was to ask for what purpose he had these names in his database. "Because we have contacted them to come here to Jerusalem to prepare to be the priests which will operate the temple when it stands in Jerusalem," replied the Rabbi.

"Why do you need these priests to come here to Jerusalem to study the priestly duties?" I asked the Rabbi. "Because we are going to build a temple here in the holy city and we need the priests to operate the temple," Kahana said. That statement almost lifted me off my seat. What a thrilling prospect for the future of the Jewish people, I thought.

Studying For The Priesthood

When I inquired, I learned that these men are studying the Levitical system for the temple sacrifices and worship so that they may operate as priests in a Jewish temple. The Book of Leviticus is written as a textbook for the priestly candidates. The first seven chapters of the book teach the system for sacrifices. Chapters 8, 9, and 10 give the standards for the priest. The last seventeen chapters detail the system of worship for the temple complex.

Every Jewish boy who is interested in spiritual things will start studying the Book of Leviticus from two years of age. Actually, his mother will start reading the book to him when he is two years old. The age for a member of the "priestly tribe" to qualify to be a priest is thirty. That means, a Jewish boy who meets the requirements to be a priest must study the Book of Leviticus for twenty-eight years before he actually becomes a priest.

Later, after thinking through the events of that interesting afternoon, I asked the Rabbi how anyone could know he was qualified to be a priest, since the genealogies had been destroyed in 70 A.D. Would it not be impossible to know which Jewish men were really qualified to be priests to operate the next temple? The answer the rabbi gave me was that it was through tradition, passed down from father to son, that these men were kept aware of their status.

He also said that someone would be foolish to claim to be of the priestly family if he was not truly qualified. "They have so many restrictions on them, the way they live, who they marry, how they eat, what they wear, and many other requirements laid out in their priestly manuals," Rabbi Kahana responded.

My study of things pertaining to the temple revealed

to me that there were to be 24,000 priests set aside to do *"the work of the house of the Lord"* (I Chronicles 23:4). That number is a part of the total number that King David gathered just prior to his death. Of the 38,000 Levites for service in the Lord's house, the aforementioned 24,000 were to be the priests, 6,000 were to be officers and judges, 4,000 were to be porters, and 4,000 were to play the musical instruments which David had made.

I asked the rabbi if there were that many men studying the priestly duties in Jerusalem. Kahana answered, tongue-in-cheek, "Those that talk, don't know and those that know, don't talk." Having done much research on this subject, I can report that there are very likely that many men in Jerusalem studying to operate the temple when it stands on the Temple Mount some day.

There is yeshiva after yeshiva where all the students are studying the priestly duties. In addition, there are a great number of Orthodox schools where the younger students, six years to eighteen years of age, are in a program that is preparing them to do priestly duties when they are old enough.

Priestly Garments

Knowing that there were men studying to operate the temple, I recalled from my studies that these men had to wear special clothing as they performed their duties. I turned to the rabbi and asked him about the priestly garments. He told me that they had many of these garments in storage and were making the ones needed to start temple operation.

The garments worn by the priests were to be both dignified and beautiful, as precious as the garments of royalty, according to the instructions given to Moses by

God. The Bible attaches much significance to the garments because they possess a certain holiness.

These priestly garments have special requirements. They must not be sewn, but instead are to be woven in a special manner, out of one piece of cloth, without seams. The arms are woven separately, and these can be attached by sewing them to the rest of the garment.

There were three categories of priestly garments. First, the High Priest's apparel that was worn all year round, consisting of eight garments called the *golden garments*. Second, the clothing worn by the High Priest on the Day of Atonement, consisting of four garments called the *white garments*. And third, the uniform of the ordinary priest, consisting of four garments. These four garments, worn all year by the ordinary priest, were identical to the "white garments" worn by the High Priest on the Day of Atonement.

The *ephod*, a sort of apron worn on the top of the other garments of the High Priest, was one of the most important of all his garments. The *breastplate* was fastened to the ephod with golden chains attached to the two square gold settings fixed on the shoulders of the High Priest. The breastplate was square-shaped and worn over the heart of the High Priest.

It was called the "breastplate of judgment, or decision," because of the unique role it played in helping to render fateful decisions for the Jewish people. Those decisions were made manifest through the stones attached to the breastplate. There were twelve stones on the breastplate, four rows of three stones each, with each stone representing one of the twelve tribes of Israel. The name of each tribe was engraved on one of the stones.

Each priest, including the High Priest, had to wear a headdress. The High Priest would wear a *turban* placed on his head in such a way to allow for the *crown* to be worn as part of his attire. There are many scholars who hold that the ordinary priests' hats were exactly the same as that of the High Priest, except the ordinary priests had their hats wound on them and the High Priest simply had his turban placed on his head.

The garment had a *sash*, made of white linen, which was placed around the waist. This belt was wrapped many times around the body. Its purpose was to separate the upper body from the lower body, required by Jewish law during prayer or the mention of anything holy.

The priests wore no shoes or sandals in their service to the temple. They would actually walk barefoot on the marble floors of the temple courts. This was done to preserve the sanctity not only of the temple itself, but also of the entire temple complex.

Many of these garments have been made and are now in storage in Jerusalem. Even as I write this, there are other garments being made, which will be used by the priests who are preparing to perform their duties in the coming temple.

Chapter 19
Implements, Instruments, and The Institute

I was satisfied that there was much activity going on among those who believe a temple must be built on the Temple Mount in Jerusalem. But because I am a journalist, I had to ask the rabbi the next logical question: "What about the implements which have to be available to operate the temple?"

Even before I could get the entire question out, the rabbi told me that they had all of the implements needed to start operation of the temple. He said that the Temple Institute, a group of dedicated Orthodox Jews who are on the cutting edge in all preparations for the next temple, had these implements in storage. I was invited to visit their institute and inspect their work.

The Temple Institute is made up of Biblical scholars and artisans. The scholars do research on those items needed to operate the temple. The artisans are then commissioned to build the implements needed. Their work has been meticulous in preparing these implements.

Those implements already prepared for temple service include the crown for the High Priest, the menorah, the table for the shewbread, the altar of incense, the mizrach, the lots for the scapegoat, and other instruments to be used by the priest. The Temple Institute now has these items on display in the Old City of Jerusalem for the purpose of allowing the priestly candidates to acquaint themselves with them.

Temple Implements

On one of my many visits to the Institute, I was

given an explanation of some of these instruments. A Jewish man who will be one of the future priests at the coming temple was on duty and explained to me the requirements for the implements and the form of service each of these items will be used for.

The *crown* for the High Priest is made out of 24-karat gold and is designed to fit the head of the one designated by the Sanhedrin as the High Priest. This is done by attaching a blue cord to the open-ended crown. The reason for using 24-karat gold is because of the softness of that weight of gold. The crown must be pliable enough to form to the headdress of the High Priest.

There is the possibility that the original *menorah* is in the basement of the Vatican in Rome, Italy. The thinking is that General Titus and the Roman Army carried it back to Rome after destroying the temple in 70 A.D. In Rome, a relief on the Arch of Titus indicates the menorah was included in those implements captured by the Romans during the war.

Because of that possibility, the Israeli government dispatched the Minister of Religious Affairs to Rome in 1996 to ask the Pope to either confirm or deny their possession of the menorah. The Pope would neither confirm nor deny, but did hint that he may return the menorah to Israel some day.

The Temple Institute, not wanting to rely on the decision of the Pope on this matter, has made a menorah to be used in the next temple. The artisans at the Institute built this full-size menorah from a model they had on display for many years. They gold-plated the menorah with 90 pounds of pure gold. Ready to stand in the temple when it is built in Jerusalem, this menorah is on display, under lock-and-key, in the Cardo in the Old City of Jerusalem.

The unique shape of the *table of shewbread* has been the subject of much study at the Temple Institute. The preparation of the bread placed in the table has been a mystery for the scholars to unfold, as well. The Institute, however, not only has the design for the shewbread table, they have constructed it for use in the temple. They also have the special formula for preparing the bread, twelve loaves that must be in the table of shewbread. As far as these items are concerned, they are ready to move ahead with the operation of the temple.

A very important implement that is essential for the operation of the temple is the *mizrach*. In fact, there are many mizrach that must be available to the priest for the daily sacrifices, as well as for the Jewish festivals, which take place each year. Some of these implements can be made of pure silver and some of pure gold.

The structure of the mizrach is such that there is no base for the pitcher-shaped implement. That is so the mizrach cannot be set down by the priest during his administration of sacrificial duties. Should he set the mizrach down—which contains the blood of goats, lambs, or bulls—the blood could clot and become contaminated.

During the Feast of Passover there will be a need for a great number of mizrach to be used by the priest to fulfill the Levitical requirements for the Passover sacrifice. Throughout history, the magnitude of the Passover feast has resulted in a large number of priests participating, using hundreds of these mizrach. The Institute has a number of mizrach, but is continuing to produce more.

There are other implements that must be used in the operation of the next temple. The *silver cup* and the *golden flask*, created by the researchers and craftsman at the Institute must be used in the ceremony of the water libation. The *incense chalice*, which holds the ingredients for the incense offering, is available for service, with all the different incense to be used, as well.

The very first service performed by the priest in the temple every day, with the first rays of dawn, was the removal of the ashes left on the altar. A *silver shovel*, always kept on the southwest corner of the altar, is now on hand for those daily needs. Another vessel needed for use by the High Priest on the Day of Atonement is the *lottery box* which contains the "lots" that are to be cast to determine which of the goats would be designated the "scapegoat."

Before the priests can tend to the offerings on the altar, they must sanctify their hands and feet with water from the *copper washbasin*. This reconstructed washbasin is at the Temple Institute awaiting service at the temple. The *silver trumpets* fashioned after Talmudic sources and the relief from the Arch of Titus, in Rome, are on display today, but stand ready for a priest to sound forth during the sacrificial service.

All of the aforementioned implements are prepared, stored, and awaiting the building of the temple. Anyone can inspect these implements at the Temple Institute in the old city of Jerusalem. There are enough implements to start the temple operation today.

Chapter 20
The Harps

Listening to Rabbi Kahana explain the activities of the Jewish people making preparations to build the temple, I could not resist asking him about the need for a large Levite orchestra to play for the worship services in the coming temple. I had studied about the previous temples and knew of this orchestra; and in fact, that they needed a large number of harps as instruments in the group.

When I asked the rabbi, "What about that?" he told me to go over to number 10 on King David Street in Jerusalem. My first response was that the name and number given me was a great address. Right away, I made my way to the address and met Micha and Shushanna Harrari. Micha and Shushanna had moved to Israel a few years earlier to make aliya. Micha had been a "finish carpenter" and, for pleasure, had once made a guitar.

One day Shushanna asked Micha to make her a harp for her upcoming birthday. Micha's first response was that he did not know how to build a harp, since he had never done that before. Shushanna immediately started to push Micha for him to grant her birthday wish for a harp. Eventually, Micha made his way to the Jezreel Valley in the center part of the state of Israel and found a picture of a 10-string harp that was carved on the wall of a cave near Megiddo.

Retrieving the image, Micha came back to Jerusalem and began work on the harp. Patterned after the cave carving, he handcrafted the harp for his wife. When the harp was completed, the Harraris were contacted by a *Jerusalem Post* reporter who wanted to interview them for a feature story in the newspaper. She wrote the story and had it published, but found herself fascinated with the instruments and so continued her research on harps.

First Harp In Years

What she discovered was that the harp that Micha had made was the first harp made in almost two thousand years in Israel. The need for harps had diminished with the destruction of Herod's Temple in 70 A.D. While the temples were standing in Jerusalem, the High Priest followed the request of King David for this large orchestra to play for the worship activities (I Chronicles 23:5).

This large orchestra was to be made up of cymbals, psalteries, trumpets, and harps. It has been determined that the larger number of these 4,000 Levites who were to serve in the temple orchestra were to play harps. This means that there must be someone in Israel producing these harps. Now for the first time in two thousand years in Israel, someone— Micha Harrari—is making Biblical harps. In fact, the Temple Institute has commissioned Micha to produce all of the harps needed for the Levite orchestra that will perform on the Temple Mount, when the temple is in full operation in Jerusalem.

Just a short while after the story about the 10-string harp ran in the *Jerusalem Post*, an elderly rabbi showed up at the Harrari Harp Studio and wanted to know if they really did have such a harp. As Shushanna showed the old rabbi the harp, he asked if he could hold the harp. Standing there clutching the harp, the rabbi started to cry. Shushanna quickly asked the rabbi if everything was all right, to which he answered that it was.

The rabbi then explained why he was shedding tears. He said that the Talmud (extra-Biblical writings for the Jewish people) records the old Jewish tradition that when a 10-string harp shows up in Jerusalem, that would be the time of the coming of the Messiah. Then it hit Shushanna that it would be their destiny, the making of these 3,000 harps needed for the operation of the temple when it stands on the Temple Mount in Jerusalem.

Chapter 21
The Lost Ark

Some say that the ark is not lost after all. They say the ark can be found exactly where it was placed over twenty-five hundred years ago. Even though there has been much talk, much written material, and much intrigue about the whereabouts of the ark, its whereabouts can be known. The ark, which was the center of Jewish worship for two thousand years, will be a part of the temple in the future, at least the temple which will be standing in Jerusalem during the seven-year Tribulation Period.

Much has been written about the ark being in Ethiopia. That rumor came about as a result of the visit to King Solomon by the Queen of Sheba, around 1000 B.C. The story goes that the King was infatuated with the Queen and gave her the ark to take back home. The ark, ending up in Ethiopia almost three thousand years ago, has been handed down through the royal families for protection to the present day.

There have even been some reports that the Ethiopians who immigrated to Israel in 1991 during Operation Solomon secretly brought the ark to the Jewish people in Israel. Those reports are baseless, according to all my investigation. The truth is that the ark never left the land of Israel once it was carried into the land by the Israelites under their leader Joshua at the time of the conquest of the Promised Land.

Proof of this statement is found in the Bible and in extra-Biblical Jewish writings. The Talmud states that the ark is in the location where the Levites carried it when instructed to take it to the secluded, secure place that King Solomon had prepared for the protection of this very sacred piece of furniture.

Where Is The Ark?

The Bible confirms the location of the ark in the account recorded in II Chronicles 35:3. This portion of the Scriptures gives the details of the times prior to the dispersion of the Jewish people during the Babylonian captivity. The ruler of Judah, King Josiah, knowing the times in which he was living, realized that the temple would come under attack when, and if, the Babylonians should come to conquer the Jewish people.

King Josiah instructed the Levites to take the ark and *"put [it] in the house"* (II Chronicles 35:3). He was not referring to the temple when he used the word "house," but the place that King Solomon had previously prepared to keep the ark safe. I have concluded that this is correct for two reasons. First, the ark had been in the "house"(or temple) for almost four hundred years at the time of this event in history. King Solomon built the temple and placed the ark in the "Holy of Holies" around 1000 B.C. (I Kings 8:1-11).

Second, the word used for "house" in Hebrew is "bayith," which means a special place, a shelter, in the inward parts. It is referring to a location which was under the "Holy of Holies" and today is found underneath the Dome of the Rock on the Temple Mount. The Talmud stated that the ark can be found there. It is this statement in the Talmud that led two rabbis to search for the lost ark in 1982.

Eyewitness Accounts

Two very prestigious rabbis decided to see if the stories from the Bible were true. When I say they were very prestigious rabbis, that is exactly what they were. Rabbi Shlomo Goren was the chief rabbi of the Israeli Defense Force in 1967. On June 7, when they took back the Old City of Jerusalem, including the Western Wall, Rabbi Goren offered the first prayer at the wall in hundreds of years. He also was the first to blow a shofar at the reclaimed Western Wall.

Rabbi Yehuda Getz was appointed as the chief rabbi of the Jewish holy sites in Israel. That responsibility included the Western Wall among all the holy sites to the Jewish people. Rabbi Getz was so important that the Orthodox Jewish leadership gave him the synagogue closest to the original "Holy of Holies."

In 1982 these two rabbis decided to go under the Temple Mount to see if the ark was really there. They broke through the Western Wall at the "Warren Gate." Walking through this uncharted area, they claim to have seen the Ark of the Covenant. Rabbi Getz told me of the sighting of the ark in an interview for my documentary on the Third Temple, "Ready to Rebuild." A television production company, producing a "prime time" special for the CBS television network, purchased the rights to that interview from me.

That same production company also commissioned me to interview Rabbi Goren on his experience with the ark. The rabbi told me that he had come within twenty-five feet of touching the most important piece of temple furniture. He said he could have brought the ark out from under the Temple Mount. I asked him why he didn't bring the ark out, to which he replied, "We will bring the ark out from its hiding place when there is some place to put the ark."

Both of these rabbis, Yehuda Getz and Shlomo Goren, have now died, but have passed along their findings to associates who know the exact whereabouts of the ark, which will be brought out and placed in the "Holy of Holies" at the appropriate time.

Chapter 22
The Sanhedrin

As a journalist stationed in Jerusalem, I have received requests to do special production assignments for various television operations, production houses, networks, and individuals interested in television footage of some kind or another. Several years ago, one such request came from a production house that was preparing a "prime time" special for CBS television.

They wanted an interview with the very distinguished Rabbi Shlomo Goren, the rabbi who was the first to offer a prayer at the Western Wall on June 7, 1967, after the Israeli Defense Force had captured the Old City of Jerusalem for the first time in almost two thousand years. It wasn't his experiences at the Western Wall at the conclusion of the Six-Day War that they wanted me to speak to him about, but his search for the "Ark of the Covenant" back in 1982.

Having finished the interview, I released the cameraman and followed the rabbi to a room, which he wanted to show me. At the door of that room, which was filled with overstuffed chairs, I—for no particular reason—started counting the chairs in the room and came up with a count of seventy chairs. The rabbi interrupted my daydreaming with, "Do you know what this room is to be used for?" I quickly snapped back, "Is this the room for the Sanhedrin?"

The rabbi's answer was a soft-spoken, "Yes." My heart skipped a beat as I regained my composure so that I could ask, "Do you have the men who will serve in the Sanhedrin?" The rabbi responded, "Yes, we do have the men who are qualified to serve in the

Sanhedrin." I then called for my cameraman for the purpose of recording a short interview with the rabbi from the room for the Sanhedrin.

Are We Ready?

With the rabbi seated in one of the seventy chairs, I repeated my questions, "Is this the room for the Sanhedrin?" "Yes," replied the rabbi. "Do you now have the men that could serve in the Sanhedrin?" "We do have the men qualified to serve in the Sanhedrin, right now," the rabbi said, as he looked across the room and out the window toward the Temple Mount. Then, my most important question, "If this is the room for the Sanhedrin, and you have the men to serve in the Sanhedrin, are you now ready to elect the High Priest to lead the services at the temple?"

I will give you his answer to that question, but first, a brief explanation about the group called the Sanhedrin is in order. The word "Sanhedrin" comes from the Greek word "synedrion," meaning a "council" or "meeting place." In the Scriptures, it refers to the governing body or supreme council for the Jews, which functioned as a religious and civil court. The people would go on the Temple Mount to have their questions answered or their causes heard and decided by the smaller Sanhedrin of twenty-three that sat at the entering of the gate or by the Greater Sanhedrin.

The power of the Sanhedrin would, of course, vary with political circumstances, being at times almost absolute while at other times it was shorn of all ecclesiastical authority. The Sanhedrin was in full force at the time of Jesus. It was an institution that exerted decisive influence on the future of Israel. They made legal determinations that the traditionalists declared absolutely binding on all, and of greater obligation than Scripture itself made. For example, "The sayings of the elders have more weight than those of the prophets." And again, "An offense against the sayings of the Scribes is worse than one against the Scripture."

The Sanhedrin can be traced back to seventy men who were appointed by Moses to assist him. In the time of Jesus, it was comprised of seventy-one members: seventy elders and scribes, and a High Priest. This group usually met near the temple in Jerusalem. The Sanhedrin could issue sentences, but only the Roman procurator could ratify and carry out a death sentence. The Great Sanhedrin in Israel exercised supreme spiritual authority and in that capacity ultimately settled all religious questions—at least for a time. The Sanhedrin was finally dismantled when Jerusalem fell in 70 A.D.

Meeting At The Temple

One other qualification for the Sanhedrin is that they must meet within the confines of the temple complex. It is a fact that the room prepared by Rabbi Goren's people is not now located within the confines of the temple, or even for that matter on the Temple Mount. But that is not a problem, because the temple that will be built next will be included in the one square mile that the Prophet Ezekiel described as the boundaries for the coming Temple Mount (Ezekiel 42:20).

The present size of the Temple Mount is approximately the size of three football fields. The size of the entire Old City of Jerusalem today is about one square mile, the exact size of the coming temple complex area called for by the prophetic Scriptures. Though the people preparing to build the temple are actually preparing to build another temple, other than the one described in Ezekiel 40–46, they do want to follow the Scriptures as closely as possible. Therefore, the Goren room for the Sanhedrin will be on the "official" Temple Mount.

The other problem for those preparing to build the next temple is that in the temple described in Ezekiel's prophecy there is no need for the Sanhedrin to elect the High Priest. Jesus Christ will be the "High Priest" for Messiah's Temple.

Now for the answer to the question I asked the rabbi there in the meeting place for the present-day Sanhedrin. Without any hesitation the rabbi told me that the Sanhedrin was ready to elect the High Priest for the coming temple. This statement meant that the people preparing to build the temple are ready to do everything that is required for the operation of the coming temple.

Chapter 23
The Ashes of the Red Heifer

One of the most talked–about subjects when it comes to the rebuilding of the temple in Jerusalem is the "ashes of the red heifer." I was first made aware of the need for these ashes, when I was interviewing one of the rabbis working with the Temple Institute. At the time of the interview, Rabbi Chaim Richman served as spokesman for the Institute, in addition to his writings and research projects for the Institute.

In the interview, the rabbi brought to my attention that we are living in a generation of spiritual awakening, especially among the Jewish people. Indeed, if you stop to think about it, we today are seeing things that other generations only dreamed about: the establishment of the state of Israel; the ingathering of so many of the Jewish Diaspora (those Jews living outside of Israel for the last two thousand years); the resurrection of a dead language (Hebrew); and a renewed interest in rebuilding the temple. Those things dreamed about in the past have come true today.

It is a time when the hand of God can be seen in the lives of mankind, by all those who are interested in seeing. As I sit at my computer writing this book, I see all around me what is happening in Israel, among the Jewish people. After almost two thousand years, the Jewish people are moving toward the time when the temple on Mount Moriah—the prophesied Third Temple—will be rebuilt.

The leaders of the world are working diligently, trying to bring together a comprehensive peace between the Israelis and their Arab neighbors. The Bible gives us the only solution for the elusive peace we all desire to see. The ancient Jewish Prophet Haggai stated that the Creator Himself, the Supreme Author of peace has promised: *"The glory of this latter house shall be greater than of the former, saith the Lord of hosts: and in this place will I give peace, saith the Lord of hosts"* (Haggai 2:9).

The Jewish mindset, for those making the actual preparations, is that they must build the temple so that the Messiah can come to rule the world from Jerusalem, sitting in His rebuilt house of worship. We have discussed many of the preparations being made for the operation of the temple, but there is one missing factor as these Jews see it: the ashes of the red heifer. These ashes must be available for the purification of the actual building, the implements, and the priests themselves.

Rabbi Chaim Richman told me, "In our times, the commandment of the red heifer takes on more and more significance. The fate of the entire world depends on the red heifer. God has ordained that its ashes alone are the single missing ingredient for the reinstatement of Biblical purity—and thereafter, the rebuilding of the Holy Temple." Those are very strong words, howbeit, from the lips of an Orthodox Jewish rabbi.

Ordinance Of The Red Heifer

The origins of the red heifer go back almost thirty-five hundred years, to the time of the Exodus. The children of Israel had been led by Moses to Mount Sinai, where the Lord was going to give His people the Torah, the written Jewish law from God. While Moses was on the mountain receiving the Law, the Israelites were in the valley making an idol in the form of a golden calf. The precept of the red heifer was given by

God following the debacle of the golden calf. God decreed that since Israel made a calf out of their gold, they should bring the funds for the red heifer.

This Jewish ordinance was recorded by Moses in Numbers 19. Though some parts of the directive dealing with the red heifer are simple enough, there are some very puzzling aspects to this ordinance. I have spent many hours studying the subject, and a good amount of time talking with the rabbis about it, and still have trouble understanding it completely. My only comfort comes from the fact that Rabbi Richman admits to the same troubles of understanding as well.

What we can understand is that a heifer (a cow which has never given birth to a calf), red in color (without more than two hairs of any other color), and never having had a yoke on her neck, was to be brought to Moses for the ceremony. The priest was to then lead the red heifer out of the tabernacle, later the temple complex, to the east of the transportable worship center to an altar that could be seen by the High Priest back at the tabernacle.

At this altar to the east of the tabernacle, the priest was to ceremonially slaughter the red heifer with a swift thrust of his knife. The dead red heifer was then to be reduced to ashes in a fire made out of cedar wood. As that process was taking place, the priest was to throw on the burning red heifer some hyssop and a piece of scarlet ribbon. Why they were to use these three items with the red heifer—cedar, hyssop, and scarlet ribbon—is part of the ordinance that neither the rabbis nor I understand.

Then, using the ashes from the red heifer, the cedar wood, the hyssop, and the scarlet ribbon, the priest mixes this solution with "running water" and stores the mixture in a stone pot until needed for purification purposes. The process of purification would be accomplished by sprinkling the ashen-water mixture on the person, or object, which was impure. Again, another puzzling aspect of the ordinance is how this water mixture would purify someone or something, aside from being obedient to God's directive.

That is how the ordinance began at the time of Moses and the children of Israel at Mount Sinai, one year after the exodus from Egyptian bondage. The ordinance was to be a *"perpetual statute"* unto the Jewish people (Numbers 19:21). And so it was until the time of the second temple, better known as Herod's Temple. This was the temple that stood in Jerusalem at the time of Jesus Christ.

In The Time Of Jesus

During those days, the red heifer ordinance was done in almost the same fashion as the Jewish people did it in the wilderness wanderings. With the permanent worship center on Mount Moriah, the priests built a bridge leading out of the Eastern Gate, across the Kidron Valley to the Mount of Olives, to the altar "outside the camp" where the slaughter of the red heifer would take place. All the other directives of the ordinance were the same and must be followed.

With the destruction of Herod's Temple by the Roman Army under General Titus, in 70 A.D., the need for these ashes and the purification process was set aside. But now with the renewed interest in the temple, those making ready everything for the coming temple also have to be prepared with the ashes of the red heifer.

At first there were those who believed some of the original ashes must be found, and added to the new ashes from a modern-day red heifer. In fact, that is still believed to be true by many who are working with the

Third Temple project. However, Rabbi Chaim Richman, most probably the world's leading scholar on the red heifer, says, "Obtaining some of the ashes from the original ashes would truly be a most fortunate turn of events."

"The truth be known," says Rabbi Richman in his book, *The Mystery of the Red Heifer*, "there is nothing to stop the people of Israel from raising a new red heifer, from birth, and preparing it in the manner described—even without the original ashes. On the contrary, we may be in doubt as to the true nature of any discovery that is unearthed whose authenticity cannot be completely verified. But a perfect heifer, born and raised under a controlled environment, would be fit to be used for the temple. And that is precisely what is being done today."

Even though Rabbi Richman has given this rabbinical ruling pertaining to the ashes of the next red heifer, there are still those who disagree with the rabbi. These people believe that there must be a recovery of some of the original ashes, to be mixed with the ashes of the newest red heifer, for the ordinance to be Biblical. One of those searching for the original ashes is a friend of mine, Dr. Gary Collett.

Search For The Ashes

Dr. Collett has been working for years on a project at Qumran in the Dead Sea area. He believes that under the plateau where the Dead Sea scrolls were found there are many artifacts, possibly including the original red heifer ashes. Though Dr. Collett was allowed to make an exploratory dig at Qumran, he has been continually hampered in his quest to find these ashes by Israeli bureaucratic hold-ups.

Most of the evidence for Dr. Collett's belief that the

ashes are under the plateau at Qumran comes from an interpretation of a passage in the Copper Scroll, one of the well-known and most cryptic Dead Sea Scrolls, discovered in one of the Qumran caves in 1952. Many believe that the Copper Scroll was authored by members of the Essene community at the close of the Second Temple period. These Essenes were the scribes who copied the original Dead Sea Scrolls.

There are those who claim to have discovered "linguistic" evidence that proves Qumran is the site described in the Copper Scroll. The Copper Scroll refers to the "Wadi HaKippah" and "Cave #4" as the entrance described in the Copper Scroll, both definite locations at Qumran.

The scroll also relates that the vessels and treasures, as well as a container of ashes of the red heifer, were taken from the temple before the destruction and hidden in the Qumran area.

Even though Dr. Gary Collett is continuing his effort to do an archeological dig at Qumran, there is no absolute evidence that the original ashes of the red heifer will be found at Qumran or anywhere else for that matter. Meanwhile, Rabbi Chaim Richman is moving forward with what he claims to be an authentic red heifer.

We are not talking about the red heifer known as "Melody," the one the world media promoted several years ago as the authentic red heifer. Melody, born on a religious youth village at Kfar Hasidim (near Haifa, Israel), though thought at first to be a red heifer that would qualify as the one needed for the ordinance, was found to have at least three hairs of a color other than red.

A Red Heifer Today

We are talking about a red heifer that Rabbi Richman has thoroughly inspected, and pronounced to be a "red heifer." The details behind the discovery of this red heifer by Rabbi Richman are a story made for television, or the movies. It begins at a farmhouse in the state of Mississippi.

The story begins on a spring evening back in 1989. A cattle breeder named Clyde Lott was sitting at his desk at home in Canton, Mississippi, studying Scriptures. On that particular night Clyde was working through the thirtieth chapter of Genesis. Verses 31 and 32 refer to Jacob's *"speckled and spotted cattle."* The idea of spotted and speckled cattle being the foundation of the continuing herd of the Israelites from their time in Egypt, the crossing of the Red Sea, and after forty years of wandering in the wilderness, ultimately accompanying the Jewish people across the Jordan River and into the land of Israel, puzzled him.

Clyde Lott, having been involved in the cattle business for so many years, began to think about the famed red heifer of Numbers 19, and questioned how a red cow could be produced on a consistent basis out of this foundation of spotted cattle. He wondered where the people of Israel obtained the red cows that were slaughtered and burned for their ashes in accordance with the laws of ritual purification.

Because of Clyde Lott's background, being a graduate of Mississippi State University who had majored in Animal Sciences and head of his family livestock operation, he decided to see if he could breed a pure red heifer. He had raised, bred, and developed several hundred different types of cattle, some of which were judged national champions. But, to breed a red heifer—was that possible? His work was cut out for him.

Clyde knew that Israel could not have a perpetual supply of red heifers. As a student of prophecy, he also knew that the preparations for the Third Temple would require the ashes of a red heifer. Where had the red heifers of the past come from? Where would the ones in the future be found? How close was Israel to obtaining a red heifer? These were all questions that Clyde wanted to get answered.

To make a long story somewhat shorter, let me tell you that Clyde Lott sent off a letter with his questions to the United States Embassy's agricultural attaché in Athens, Greece. Though the embassy's agricultural desk in Greece was responsible for the entire Middle East, after reading the letter, the office in New York City forwarded the letter to the United States Embassy in Tel Aviv, Israel. They in turn sent it to the Ministry of Religious Affairs for the State of Israel in Jerusalem. They sent the same letter to the Temple Institute, where it finally arrived on the desk of Rabbi Chaim Richman—after traveling around the world for ninety days.

This letter from an inquisitive cattle breeder in Canton, Mississippi would get a personal response from the rabbi. In fact, it was this letter that brought these two men from very different backgrounds together for this special project, the breeding of an authentic red heifer. Clyde would endeavor to develop a pure red heifer that would meet the requirements set forth in the Bible for the animal to be sacrificed on the Mount of Olives, in Jerusalem.

The Rabbi's Inspection

Rabbi Richman finally made a trip to Canton,

Mississippi, to inspect the red heifers bred and raised by cattleman Clyde Lott. On the afternoon that the rabbi arrived at the Lott farm in Canton, Mississippi, Clyde had washed and groomed the four heifers he wanted the rabbi to inspect. The rabbi had to inspect the heifers thoroughly: the skin, the hoofline, the eyebrows, and even the ears. Finally, after studying one heifer for almost ten minutes, he stepped back and said something to Clyde and his brother.

"This is the heifer that will change the world," Rabbi Richman said to the Lott brothers. He told them that this heifer, standing in front of him, one that Clyde Lott had bred, met all the Biblical requirements of Numbers 19. This was the first time in two thousand years that a red heifer had been verified by a rabbi, meeting all the requirements.

The Tenth Red Heifer

In a later conversation with the rabbi at Clyde's farm in Canton, he told me something that thrilled me. The rabbi told one of the most interesting facts about the appearance of a qualified red heifer. In his studies on the red heifer, his research revealed to him that from the time of the first red heifer in Moses' day until the last one at the time of the destruction of the Second Temple, there had been only nine red heifers.

The rabbi had documented this information with the names of the High Priests who had prepared the nine red heifers. Rabbi Richman said the great Jewish scholar, Maimonides, when recounting the historic record of the nine red heifers, wrote in his commentary to the Mishna, extra-Biblical Jewish writings, these comments, "And the tenth red heifer will be accomplished by the king, the Messiah; may He be revealed speedily, Amen, May it be God's will."

The Jewish people, expecting the rebuilding of the Third Temple in the near future, now have a qualified red heifer for use as a sacrificial offering in purification rituals. The Jewish tradition is that when a tenth red heifer shows up, it is the time for the coming of the Messiah. The tenth red heifer is here. Can the coming of the Messiah be far behind?

Chapter 24
Think About This!

The next event in God's calendar is the Rapture of the Church, when people who know Jesus Christ as their Lord and Saviour will be called to meet Him in the air. Heralded by three heavenly sounds—the shout of the archangel, Jesus calling, and the sound of the trumpet—believers will be called to be with Him, forevermore.

Sometime after the Rapture, we're not sure how long a period of time it will be, the seven-year Tribulation Period will begin. The beginning of those seven years will be marked by the confirmation of a peace treaty between Israel, the Antichrist, and the enemies of the Jewish nation in the Middle East. At the end of the Tribulation Period, the trumpet will sound again and the Messiah will return to the earth, coming down to the Mount of Olives in Jerusalem.

These two events will bookend the Tribulation: the Rapture of the Church and the Return of Christ. Both will be announced with a trumpet blast from Heaven.

This book has been about what will happen between those two glorious events; the time between those two trumpet blasts. I have shared with you four trends that will provide visible signs of the end times; trends foretold by Biblical prophets long ago. Apparent in our world today, these trends give us evidence as to how close we may be to the first of those trumpet sounds. It is not idle speculation to look at current events in light of the Biblical scenario for the last days, as recorded by the ancient Jewish prophets.

Trend 1: *Aliya*

Never before in the history of the world has there been such a flow of Jewish people into Israel from all the different nations of the world. It has been interesting to note the large groups that have arrived in Israel in the last decade alone. These Jews come from nations mentioned by prophets who wrote over twenty-five hundred years ago. The prophets were very specific in naming the nations that would be in the spotlight in the last days.

I cannot walk through the streets of Jerusalem without being able to reach out and actually touch at least the partial fulfillment of prophecy. Every day I mingle with Ethiopian and Russian Jews who have recently returned to the land of their forefathers. Traveling in and out of Israel as I do, it is impossible not to notice the new immigrants arriving almost daily in the land. This aliya is certainly a trend that one must take notice of in these days.

Trend 2: *Alignment*

You cannot pick up the newspaper, listen to the radio, or watch television without seeing or hearing something about one of the nations mentioned in this book. As we've discussed, these nations will be at the forefront of the alignment of nations that God says will come against Israel in the end times. Every report seems to indicate that each of these nations is working to put itself in a better position to fulfill the game plan God laid out for His Will to be accomplished on the world stage.

No matter how hard the United Nations, the European Parliament, or any governmental body may try to keep the nations from going to war, they can't seem to stop the forming of coalitions put together to attack what is perceived as the "enemy." In fact, the United Nations has become an arena for the enemies of Israel and the Jewish people to launch their verbal attacks.

This verbal communication then becomes that which will incite others to action against Israel. Over one-third of all the resolutions passed in the United Nations are aimed at the state of Israel. The nations first line up against Israel in the halls of government and then on the battlefields in the Middle East.

Trend 3: *Anticipation*

While all of the rhetoric is being spewed out against Israel at the United Nations, many of these same national leaders are trying to put together a "comprehensive peace agreement" for Israel and its neighbors. It seems as if the world leaders are standing in line to be a part of the "final" peace agreement. They fly in and out of the Middle East to negotiate for the two parties. "Shuttle diplomacy" is a worn-out phrase that has yet to really work.

Ironically, there are already peace agreements on the table that are not working as designed. Day after day there is this consistent cry for someone to come on the scene that can make these peace accords really work. How interesting it is to see that what is happening in the peace process is that which the ancient Jewish prophets said would happen. Peace treaties have been signed, but they need someone to strengthen them, make them stronger, to actually confirm these peace agreements for the sake of all parties.

Trend 4: *Arrangements*

In the midst of all this political activity, there is an effort to return to the days of the temple worship and sacrifices. Though there is only a small minority of religious Jews that are intently preparing to rebuild the temple on the Temple Mount in Jerusalem, these actions have caught the notice of the world.

If you study the Scriptures that relate to the temple, you will find out that there are at least two temples in the future. The Prophet Ezekiel describes a temple that will stand on the Temple Mount in Jerusalem during the millennial kingdom where the Messiah, Jesus Christ, will rule and reign. This temple is called "Messiah's Temple."

However, Daniel, in his prophecy about the seven-year Tribulation Period, reveals the presence of a temple standing in Jerusalem before the Messiah comes to set up His kingdom (Daniel 9:27). Jesus Christ confirms Daniel's prophecy while teaching the disciples about the end of time in the Olivet Discourse (Matthew 24:15). Both of these references are to a temple in the time of the Tribulation.

The Apostle Paul speaks of the same time period and also a temple in Jerusalem where the Antichrist will enter and set himself up as God (II Thessalonians 2:4). This is evidence that the temple in the Tribulation is a "false" temple for a "false" messiah. The Book of Revelation, the book that describes the entire period of the seven-year Tribulation (Revelation 4:2–19:10), confirms that there will be a temple in Jerusalem during the Tribulation (Revelation 11:1-2).

These Jewish activists are almost ready to build the next temple right now. Since we know that it is the temple for the Tribulation Period and not the Messiah's

Temple for the millennial kingdom, then how close must we be to the Rapture of the Church, which happens before the actual construction work on the temple begins?

Think About This!

I must remind you that I do not know when the Lord Jesus Christ will come back for the Church at the Rapture. But I do know it could happen at any moment, for there is not one other thing that must happen before this event takes place, according to the Scriptures. Those trends which will be in play during the Tribulation, are very actively in play right now. This is a period of time unprecedented in history.

Between the two trumpet sounds, the one for the Rapture and the one at the Return of Jesus, events will unfold on this earth that will give clear and unquestionable evidence for the Jewish people, so they can know the times in which they are living. God has promised the Jews a warning of the last days, before the coming of the Messiah. As we look at these four major trends, aliya of the Jewish people, alignment of the nations, anticipation for peace, and the arrangements for the temple, it is difficult not to notice how close we are to these end-time events.

And so, as we approach the end times, should we be concerned? My reason for sharing with you, through the pages of this book, my insights into Biblical prophecy is not to upset or concern you, but rather to alert you. Are you prepared for the Lord's return? If your answer is "no" or you're just not sure, then please know that getting prepared is as simple as A, B, C.

Admit that you are a sinner in need of a
  Saviour to take away your sin.

Believe that Jesus Christ died for you to take away
  that sin. Believe that He rose from the dead to
  prove He is who He said He is and can do what
  He said He would do. Believe that He will save
  you as He said He would.

Call upon Him to save you. The Bible says in
  Romans 10:13, *"Whosoever shall call upon the
  name of the Lord shall be saved."*

And with salvation comes the assurance that when
that first trumpet is blown, you'll be called up to meet
Christ and be with him forever.

The evidence in this book is revealing enough to
make anyone pause and take notice of the times that we
presently live in. The truth that cannot be denied is that
Jesus Christ could come back to earth today. The reality
of that truth should cause every one of us to strive
harder to live pure and productive lives, anticipating
the "any moment sound of trumpets."

One thing you can know for sure is that the Lord's
return is closer today than it was yesterday. Therefore,
let's keep looking up......Until.

About the Author

Dr. Jimmy DeYoung presently resides in Jerusalem, Israel. During speaking tours in the United States, South America, Africa, and Europe, Jimmy brings with him the latest news and updates from the Middle East with a unique mix of political, Biblical, and prophetic insight that can't be found in the media today.

After graduating from Tennessee Temple University, Jimmy joined with Jack Wyrtzen and Harry Bollback at Word of Life Fellowship in Schroon Lake, New York. Over the next twelve years he served in various positions with the organization, including staff evangelist, host of the Word of Life Inn, and radio program producer.

For five years Jimmy was Vice-President and General Manager of New York City's first Christian radio station, WNYM. During that time he was the producer and host of a daily talk program in the No. 1 media market in America.

Since 1991, Jimmy and his wife Judy have been residing in Jerusalem where they work as credentialed journalists in the second-most populated journalistic city in the world. Arriving there just three days before the outbreak of the Gulf War, they weathered thirty-nine Scud attacks. Undaunted, Jimmy proceeded to broadcast live reports throughout the Gulf Crisis. Today, he remains in the center of what is considered the media "hot spot" of our time, the Middle East.

More recently, Jimmy had the privilege of receiving his Doctorate from Tennessee Temple University (May 1996) and his Ph.D. from Louisiana Baptist University (May 2000).

In addition to his educational pursuits and demanding work schedule, Jimmy is a devoted husband and family man. Happily married for forty-one years, he and Judy have raised four children—Jimmy, Leslie, Jodi, and Rick—all of whom are in Christian service today. Family is a high priority for Jimmy, and these days he likes nothing better than spending time with his grandchildren.

Jimmy DeYoung is a noted prophecy teacher and conference speaker, in the United States, as well as South America, Africa, and Europe. As a part of his prophecy ministry, Jimmy has authored and produced several audio and video materials, including his best-seller video, "Ready to Rebuild," and his more recent 2-hour video, "The Daniel Papers." In his newsletter, *Until*, and weekly nationwide talk program, "Prophecy Today," Jimmy offers the most up-to-date information on current events and shares his insights on their relationship to prophecy.

Jimmy can be seen on the Day of Discovery television program and can be heard weekly on the radio with reports from the Middle East. In addition to many local talk programs, listen for Jimmy DeYoung on:

- Prophecy Today
- Prophetic Prospective
- Radio Bible Class Weekend
- Moody Broadcasting Network
- Prime Time America
- Songtime, U.S.A.
- Friends of Israel Network

For more information, view Jimmy's web site:
www.prophecytoday.com

Write or call Jimmy as follows:
PO Box 2510
Chattanooga, TN 37409
Phone: (423) 825-6247

Bennett, Ramon. *Philistine: The Great Deception.* Jerusalem: Arm of Salvation, 1979.

"The Camp David Accords: The Framework for Peace in the Middle East." Washington, D.C. September 17, 1978.

Carter, Jimmy. *Keeping Faith: Memoirs of a President.* New York: Bantam Books, 1982.

Herzl, Theodor. *The Diaries of Theodor Herzl.* [Edited and Translated, with an Introduction by Marvin Lowenthal.] Gloucester, Massachusetts: Peter Smith Publishers, 1978.

Herzl, Theodor. *The Jewish State.* Mineola, New York: Dover Publications, Inc., 1988.

Hitchcock, Mark. *After the Empire: The Fall of the Soviet Union and Bible Prophecy.* Oklahoma City: Hearthstone Publishing, 1992.

The Holy Bible. Authorized King James Version.

Josephus, Flavius. *Antiquities of the Jews.* Grand Rapids, Michigan: Kregel Publications, 1988.

Morey, Robert. *The Islamic Invasion: Confronting the World's Fastest Growing Religion.* Eugene, Oregon: Harvest House Publishers, 1992.

The Oslo Accords: "Declaration of Principles on Interim Self-Government Arrangements." Washington, D.C. September 13, 1993.

Richman, Chaim. *The Mystery of the Red Heifer: Divine Promise of Purity.* Jerusalem, 1997. Sadat, Anwar. "Address to the Israeli Knesset." November 20, 1977.

Showers, Dr. Renald E. *The Most High God.* New Jersey: Friends of Israel, 1982.

"Treaty of Peace Between the State of Israel and the Hashemite Kingdom of Jordan." Arabah Crossing Point, Israel. October 26, 1994.

Walvoord, John F. and John E. Walvoord. *Armageddon, Oil and the Middle East Crisis.* Grand Rapids, Michigan: The Zondervan Corporation, 1974.

Walvoord, John and Roy Zuck. *The Bible Knowledge Commentary: New Testament Edition.* Wheaton, Illinois: Victor Books, 1983.

Walvoord, John and Roy Zuck. *The Bible Knowledge Commentary: Old Testament Edition.* Wheaton, Illinois: Victor Books, 1983.